D1630661

THE
CENTURY
SPEAKS

BIRMINGHAM
voices

N 0160867 3

Joan Stoker and husband Ron, 2 November 1946. Their wedding reception was held at the Old Farm Inn, Bournville.

THE
CENTURY
SPEAKS

BIRMINGHAM
voices

WITHDRAWN

Memories of Birmingham people
compiled by Lucy Harland from interviews by Helen Lloyd
*for the **BBC Radio WM** series*
The Century Speaks

NEWMAN UNIVERSITY
BARTLEY GREEN
BIRMINGHAM B32 3NT
CLASS 942.496
BARCODE 01608673
AUTHOR HAR

TEMPUS

First published 1999
Copyright © BBC Radio WM, 1999

Tempus Publishing Limited
The Mill, Brimscombe Port,
Stroud, Gloucestershire, GL5 2QG

ISBN 0 7524 1848 3

Typesetting and origination by
Tempus Publishing Limited
Printed in Great Britain by
Midway Clark Printing, Wiltshire

Dedication

To Barbara and Donald Lloyd, and Janet and Robin Harland.

Derek and Bruce Bennett outside their house on Windleaves Road, Castle Bromwich, 1958.

CONTENTS

A family group, Dyche Collection.

INTRODUCTION

The people who share their memories and photographs in this book all took part in the BBC's Millennium Oral History Project, *The Century Speaks*. They were chosen because of their ability to communicate, and also because their range of ages and backgrounds would present a broad picture of local experience, opinion and knowledge.

The interviews were undertaken by Helen Lloyd between November 1998 and April 1999, to provide material for a series of documentaries on BBC Radio WM, and also to contribute to a Millennium Memory Bank at the National Sound Archive, housed in the British Library. The aim of the project was to go beyond memories of wartime and work – which have been well documented elsewhere – and to explore other aspects of daily life throughout the twentieth century. What results is an important and interesting collection of oral history interviews that range from the humorous to the intensely personal and moving.

Helen Lloyd is a freelance lecturer and radio journalist who has contributed to the

Eunice McGhie-Belgrave and her children, Lileth, Arthur, Colin and Bernadette in 1972. Eunice came to England from Jamaica in 1957 to join her first husband.

BBC's national networks and the World Service for twenty years. Her wide experience as a broadcaster is reflected in the quality and diversity of interviews now contained within this impressive archive resource for the West Midlands.

Lucy Harland has edited this selection of highlights from the interviews. She is a radio journalist and former history curator at Birmingham Museum and Art Gallery; and her choice of material reflects both her knowledge of Birmingham's past and her understanding of the present.

We hope that this book will delight equally those who have lived in the city all their lives, and those who are discovering it for the first time.

Helen Lloyd, Producer, *The Century Speaks*
Lucy Harland, Editor, *Birmingham Voices*
July 1999

An Irish fiddler plays at Larry and Nuala Finglass' wedding, March 1968.

ACKNOWLEDGEMENTS

This book could not have been produced without the generosity of the interviewees in sharing their memories and in giving us permission to print them. We are also very grateful to all those who have lent us their cherished family photographs and allowed us to reproduce them here.

We would like to thank the BBC for permission to use extracts from the interviews, and Paul Taylor and Martin Flynn of Birmingham Library Services for providing us with images from their unique photographic archive. The project would not have been possible without the help of BBC researchers, Siobhan Mullen and Emma Richardson, and volunteer researchers, Josephine Adams, Nicola Cox, Shona O'Donoghue and Azma Shain.

Lucy Harland would like to thank Grace and Peter Winckles, and Helen Lloyd would like to thank Rowland, Simon and Sarah Cotterill for their patience and support.

CHAPTER 1

Growing up

Gwen Pryke (now Webb) and her brothers
Rob, Guy and Roy in 1916. The photograph
was taken for their father who was serving in
the Army in the Middle East.

Soldiers of the Royal Warwickshire Regiment return from Italy, 1919.

Back from the War

It was 1915 when dad went. I had just about started school in the infants. He was sent off to the Middle East and it was four years before we saw him. When the fathers came home, they all came home by tram. The tram was at the top of the road and we all marched up there with our little flags and processed down the road. My father was sent out to Turkey so it was 1919 before he got home so everything had quietened down. The telegram came and mother was almost too frightened to open it. It said that he'd be on New Street Station. She took me with her to town. At New Street Station there was this bridge and there were two lots of steps on to the platform and she posted me at the bottom of one and she was at the bottom of the other. There weren't many soldiers on the train so it wasn't really difficult to look for him. Over the piano there was a photograph of him in his uniform and I had a good look at that before I came out because I'd really forgotten what he looked like. Mother, of course, knew him straight away.

Gwendoline Webb, born 1908

Home to the Shelter

There were a lot of raids over Birmingham. As soon as the raids started, the sirens went and we were all shepherded down into the basement of the school. We had to sit on long benches there. But not my brother, he would dodge and run all the way home because mum wouldn't hear the siren, being deaf. Air-raid wardens used to shout to him 'Get under cover' but he used to go all the way home. Every time there was a raid he used to go home and tell mum and then they used to go into the Anderson shelter which was in the garden.

Dan Jones, born 1929

Back Home

I was evacuated with my brother John. We were taken to Yorkshire and I was evacuated to a farm. They took to me and it was very nice. My mother was having my third brother and didn't like us being away from her so she came up and brought us back.

Bob Houghton, born 1936

The Last Boy

They came round to evacuate us. My brother didn't go because he was older. They sent me sister away first and then they sent me down to Wales. I'd never heard of Wales. We went down there on the coach. Mum was there waving us off and she was upset but I thought it was great. They took us down to Wales and we got off in wonderful mountains. We were tramping round knocking on doors but for some strange reason all they wanted was girls, so the

Dan Jones with his older brother Michael, their mother Laura and sister Betty in 1936.

girls went straight away. Then it got to 9/9.30 at night and it was dark and I was the last one, and I thought 'Crikey, nobody wants me'. I thought this was the end of the world. We knocked at this one door and the woman's name was Madame Price and she was an opera singer. She said 'I put down for a girl' and they said 'Look at him. He's the last one and it's getting on for ten o'clock'. She said 'Alright, I'll take him'.

Dan Jones, born 1929

Back from the War

My father was in the forefront of the war. When he came home from the war, he came back as a man that we never knew. My mum was always saying 'Your dad's going to come home and it's going to be great'. The day my dad arrived he came home late one evening. He came with a big kit bag. We was all geared up to see him and the first thing he said was 'Get them blasted kids to bed. What are they doing here?' Mum

Evacuees leave a school in the Midlands, 1941.

Bob Houghton's father spent time in France during the Second World War (back row, third from right).

put us to bed and he emptied his kit bag all over the floor. In the night we could hear my mum crying and shouting and it wasn't until later on that I realised he was abusing her. We heard it as children. He would hit my mum and pull her hair out. But she loved him and there was nothing we could say. He was never there. One day I was out playing and I saw him with another woman. He left mum with six children. He was violent to us. He used to hit us something terrible. He broke a piece of wood over my head all because I'd lost half a crown.

Bob Houghton, born 1936

Birmingham City

I never used to miss a match, first team or second team. It was 3d for a reserve game for me, 6d for a first team game. It was double for the men. A lot of the men used to let the lads in under their legs. They'd be queued up at the turnstile and a little lad would walk up and they'd nip him in between their legs. Twenty minutes before the end of the match, they'd open the gates and you'd see all the children flocking with bags, collecting the empty bottles to take back to get the pennies off them.

Harry Phillips, born 1922

A Bar of Cadbury's

In the '30s, you'd start off by having the Shirley Silver Band going round St Andrews. They always used to play for the first team on a Saturday. There used to be a chap who used to go round with two whippets in blue and white

Rowheath Pavillion, Bournville, 1936.

coats. He was the mascot in those days. I used to sit on the same barrier every week and that was my corner. All the chaps used to know me round there and they used to say 'Make room for the kid'. They'd sit me on the corner of the barrier and I'd have a penny bar of Cadbury's nut chocolate. A chap used to come round with the tea urn on his back and a carrier on the front with chocolate and crisps in, and you'd buy it off the tray.

Harry Phillips, born 1922

Cannon Hill

When Michael was small, I used to go up to Cannon Hill Park every morning after breakfast pushing him in the pram and then when I saw he was

going to sleep, I'd dash back home to do a bit of housework. We used to go up there when the conkers were falling off the trees and pick them up.

Sadie Bryant, born 1907

Cannon Hill Park

The one thing I loved about my granddad is that we used to go for long walks in Cannon Hill Park. From an early age I used to go for walks with my granddad right round the park. We were allowed to pick the conkers up and take them home and collect leaves for school projects. When I was studying in the early '80s, and I couldn't revise, I would go and sit in the park and just listen to groups of people who had their guitars. They would just sit there and sing and I felt very much like a hippie. In the summer holidays, when my nephews and nieces got older, we would spend every single day in the park. We would take a packed lunch. We would take our books and we would just sit in the park and play throughout the whole day. We did literally spend every summer in the park. I would take the neighbours' kids. On one occasion, I had thirteen children with me.

Avtar Tulwar, born 1969

On the Benches

Across the road from me was a big cinema and we used to go there on Saturday and for 1d we used to go and see films like *Flash Gordon*. All the seats were long benches and there were about five or six men continually shouting 'Quiet, quiet'. Every time they brought kids in, they used to shove them on the end of the seat. They shoved that many on, that they were falling off at the other end.

Alfred Palmerfield, born 1927

Rotten Fruit

Outside the cinema was a lot of handcarts loaded with fruit that they used to sell to people. We used to pick the rotten fruit up from the gutter, take it into the cinema with us and when the villain used to come on, we used to throw it at the screen.

Alfred Palmerfield, born 1927

Cannon Hill Park. Avtar Tulwar's nephews and nieces enjoy a day out in the park.

Carlton cinema, Saltley.

Coca Cola

The first time I had Coca Cola was in Coventry in the '60s. I had never had it. We used to have Tizer and Corona. Coca Cola was quite exotic. I remember my father tasting it and not liking it, so I didn't like it.

Richard Jeffs, born 1954

Playtime

I remember starting school in 1962. That was Hope Street School. I remember my mother took me into the class and there was a lot of children sat round on the floor. When my mother left me, she said to me 'When the bell goes, you come home'. So when they rang the bell for playtime, I promptly got up and went home across the road.

She was amazed 'What are you doing home?' she said. I said 'Well the bell's gone'. So she took me back.

Steve Rogers, born 1957

Walking to School

I went to school at Corpus Christi in Stechford. It must have been three or four miles and as kids we walked it because there was no money for the bus. So we walked it to school and we walked it back.

Peter Donnelly, born 1932

The First Car

About 1928, my father bought his first T-Model Ford and we used to go down to the market in that. We hadn't got any indicators, just a big white hand on a wire. When you turned left, you used to pull a lever and the big hand used to shoot up. Dad used to come to school to pick us up. We were the only ones in the district with a vehicle and all the kids used to run behind booing and shouting.

Stanley Webb, born 1916

Car Journeys

I either walk the children to school or I take them in the car. I'm very lazy, it's not that far. We should walk. It's just more convenient to take them in the car. My twelve year old, she goes anywhere she wants to go as long as her dad or I take her there or pick her up. If she's got a disco on, we take her to the disco and we fetch her from the disco. And I think my husband will be doing that until she is well into her teens.

Maria Finch, born 1963

Milk Monitor

In junior school when I was seven or eight in about 1970, we used to have a little bottle of milk every day. I was a milk monitor which meant that I used to have to dish out the milk and collect the empty bottles. Many children never drank it because they didn't like it. They used to put it near to the radiators to defrost it and it used to smell and curdle. We used to have free milk everyday which I used to love.

Maria Finch, born 1963

Richard Jeffs' class, Stanville Primary School, Sheldon, in 1963.

Vicarage Road Infant School, Aston, 1932.

Penny Biscuits

The first playtime was preceded by penny biscuits and milk. As soon as the biscuits came out, I put my hand up and asked 'Is this dinnertime, 'cause I've got to go home for me dinner'.

Richard Jeffs, born 1954

Punishment at School

I went to a good class council school. We had vicious teachers. They were brutal. One teacher used to use a ruler not a cane and hit you across the back of the neck with it. And we had another teacher who was bullied by the lads. You got the cane regular. When they hit you with the cane, they hit you.

They cut your fingers. My brother, he had the cane and he cut four of his fingers and he had to have stitches. My father being the butcher used to come down with the chopper out of the butcher's shop and chase the teachers out of the classroom.

Stanley Webb, born 1916

Comprehensive School

I wanted to go to Waverley Grammar but my parents wouldn't have any of it. They said 'All schools are going to be comprehensive very shortly. You must go to Sheldon Heath Comprehensive. It's a new one, it's been designed specially and you'll love it'. I had a lot of fun there. There was 1,200 children in the school. We liked our school to be the best. We genuinely believed that, and that's what we wanted it to be.

Richard Jeffs, born 1954

Beatings

The teacher would haul me out of the class, make me stand in the corner and he would say 'Stand with your face to the wall'. He used to put his hand on the back of my neck and his fingers would move up and down the back of my neck and he would say 'I'm going to wring this little scrawny neck of yours'. He would say 'Drop your trousers, you're going to get your bum smacked'. He happened to be our

Richard Jeffs aged twelve, not long after he started at Sheldon Heath Comprehensive.

Children listen to a story at a primary school in 1973.

The lead grate was at the heart of many homes. Blackleading the grate was a seemingly never-ending task.

swimming teacher as well and we would go swimming then he would blow his whistle and we all had to go out of the water. He would say 'The last one out of the water will get the strap' which was a big leather thong. He would make you stand on the bench where you got dressed and he'd whip your legs and he'd whip your backside with this thong. It always seemed to be me for some reason.

Bob Houghton, born 1936

A Golden Summer

I was predicted these awful grades and mum promised me, thinking I am only going to get about three GCSEs, £25 for every pass. It worked out she was going to have to dish about £200 which was one of the reasons why this summer was so great. All of my friends look back on this golden summer of '97 where anything was possible. We all went down to Highbury Park at two in the morning and we'd just indulge in conversations for hours and hours. That was such a one-off time that we will never have again.

Morgan, born 1981

Chores

I was brought up in a back-to-back house in Watery Lane. When you come home from school at night, there was a big black iron grate and twice a week, before you could go out to play, you used to have to blacklead that grate and polish the ornaments on the side and the brasses that used to sit on the

mantleshelf. You used to have to scrub the wooden table before you could go out. And you used to have to go down the cellar which was always damp and wet and get the coal and light the fire for your mum and dad.

Harry Phillips, born 1922

Helping Out

I think that children today are brought up to be the very centre of life. In our day, they had to fit in very much with the family but now everything seems to revolve around the children. We were loved but we weren't absolutely the middle of everything. When you got home from school, you were expected to do a certain amount of chores like

Joan Stoker and sister, Audrey, outside their house, 182 Woodlands Park Road, Bournville, 1928.

Norman Jeffs washes the family's A35 van on a Sunday morning.

shopping for your mother, help your father dig the garden, help with the cooking, wash up and wipe up. You were part of the family. Whereas I don't think my grandchildren have been expected to do jobs like that, although they are not spoilt.

Joan Stoker, born 1922

Doing the Ironing

My mum was very busy and my dad wasn't very well so at ten years old I was responsible for all of the housework and all of running the house. So, a typical Sunday for me would be making sure everybody's had a bath – you have your bath on Sunday – making sure all the clothes are ironed and ready for us five children. Then I'd have to get mum and dad's clothes ready for the week, especially dad as he needed to change every day. I'd make sure that he had seven trousers, seven shirts, seven vests, seven pairs of socks and my mum just knew that she could trust me to do that.

Neila Butt, born 1970

Questioning

My children do question me but I don't remember questioning my mum. She just said 'You do it' and we just did it. My children question everything. Everything I say to them, they'll say 'Why?' That could be from 'Go upstairs to get yourself washed and dressed', to 'Come on then, we're going out'. It will be 'Why Mum?' They are so independent so very, very early. They need to know the whys and wherefores of everything.

Maria Finch, born 1963

Sunday Rituals

Sundays my father would lie in and wouldn't get up 'til nine o'clock. Then we'd get up and have a good cooked breakfast with fried bread. We'd then wash the car. We'd have lunch which would be a roast and then in the afternoon my father would have forty winks. Then we'd go out and do the garden. It was always the car in the morning and the garden in the afternoon. Then we'd have afternoon tea. On Sunday nights, I would have to have a bath. Sunday night was the night you must be clean.

Richard Jeffs, born 1954

Father's Advice

My father always told us 'Work hard, study hard and you'll get everything you want'. You'd think as a child 'Gordon Bennett, he's having a go. I am never going to have a go at my children'. But I find myself saying exactly the same thing. It's a sound base because you want the best for your children.

Gurdip Gill, born 1969

Large Family

I come from a large family of six boys and six girls. My dad died very young in 1970 of lung cancer. He was a heavy smoker. My mum died last year. Being a large family, my mum lived round the corner and when you went round every day to see her there was always plenty of brothers and sisters. Since my mum

Larry Finglass with his nephews, Stephen and David, in August 1967.

Ravinder Sohal, Avtar Tulwar's older sister, and their grandfather. Avtar's grandfather played a central role in the daily life of her family.

died, we seem to have split up. There seems to be no meeting place now because we're all over Kings Heath. In the twelve months she's been gone, some of the sisters I used to see maybe two or three times a week, I haven't seen.

Larry Finglass, born 1946

Granddad

My granddad was a very forward thinking man because he wanted us all to do well. He treated us equally, boys and girls. My dad took a back seat because my granddad was seen as the head of the household. My granddad made the decisions. I remember hearing the ice cream van and saying 'Dad, can we have an ice cream?' and dad would say 'Ask granddad'. When big decisions had to be made we always discussed it with my granddad and my grandmother. In those days, it was a common factor in most Asian families that the grandparents would make the decisions.

Avtar Tulwar, born 1969

After Mother's Death

In 1976, the biggest tragedy of my life is when I lost my mother to heart failure and I was a six-year-old child. It was very difficult on the whole family. My sister left school at fifteen. She was the second eldest in the family. She looked after all of us and really took on the mother's role of bringing us up. My father worked eighteen hours a day, seven days a week to make sure we had what we wanted. We never went without. He was working in a foundry. He'd come home, have a meal and he may go back and do a night shift as well. Maybe he'd only get four or five hours sleep. Looking at my childhood in the early '70s, what I had, I appreciated. What meant more to me was playing with the other kids on the street. Now I teach my children that they are lucky. I told my son, who is five, how I lost my mother and how I did go without things. Sometimes I would cry myself to sleep. Now, since I have had children myself, I probably feel the death of my mother more. When I look at my children, I realise what I have missed.

Gurdip Gill, born 1969

The Park

We live in a cul-de-sac so I do let my children go out there and play. We can see them. We take them to the park but I wouldn't let my children go to the park on their own. It's completely out of bounds to them. The reason that I restrict my children is because you can't trust people nowadays – you hear of so many children who are abducted or attacked. The other reason is there is so much traffic, even on the quiet roads on this estate.

Maria Finch, born 1963

Playing in the Street

We weren't allowed to play in the street because mum said it was common. You weren't allowed to play on the doorstep, you could play in the garden or in the park. On this street there wasn't many Asians and my mum just wanted to make sure she knew exactly where we were.

Avtar Tulwar, born 1969

Playing out

We were allowed far more freedom than the children of today. I could pop round to the neighbours and say 'Are you coming out to play?' We'd grab a piece of skipping rope and go and play round the lamp. You could stop out until it was dusk.

Marjorie Sanders, born 1915

Henry Road

Most of our childhood was playing out of doors in Henry Road playing fields or playing out in the street with our friends and our neighbours. In those days it was a lot safer to play in the street because there were very few cars. This was in the early 1940s. There was only one family that had a car in the road. That was very posh in those days. We played football, tipcat, hopscotch, even skipping with the girls.

Peter Donnelly, born 1932

Marjorie Sanders as a girl of eight is pictured with her mother, Kate, in 1922.

Freedom

We were able to go out by ourselves. We walked down the road by ourselves whereas now children have to be taken. In many ways they've got more freedom but in other ways they've got less.

Joan Stoker, born 1922

Playing in the Street

When I was seven or eight in the early '70s, my mum was never very keen for me to play in the street. If I played with friends, they tended to come into my back garden or I would go into their back garden.

Maria Finch, born 1963

Fireball XL5

ITV started when I was two in 1955 but we didn't have ITV. By the time 1962 came round and I was taking part in street games, all these people who were in our road would want to play *Fireball XL5* because they'd all got ITV and I hadn't. I did feel left out. So I remember thinking up a marvellous line, and it worked 'Mummy, I'm an outcast at school' and I did it in my most appealing way. I came back one afternoon in about 1963 and there was a new television and it had ITV.

Richard Jeffs, born 1954

Joan Stoker aged three, wearing a sou'wester and mac bought by her aunts, in 1925. Joan had a sister fifteen months younger than herself and had to let the baby ride in the family pram. Her aunts, concerned that Joan would be exposed to the elements, bought her this outfit.

Television in the 1970s

I didn't have a television in my bedroom as my children do. I had books and a few dolls. Then as I got older, I had records and a record player. There wasn't anything on the telly during the day. It was only when I got home from school that I would watch a little bit of television. In the late '60s, early '70s, there was a programme called the *Banana Splits*. We used to watch *Andy Pandy* and *Playschool* but I didn't really watch that much television. If I didn't go out and play in the back garden or play out in the street with other kids, then I'd be in my room or I'd be doing something for my mum.

Maria Finch, born 1963

A Seventies Childhood

It was fantastic in the '70s and early '80s, playing in the street. Some of

Receipt for mending the Jeffs' television in 1962. The year after this, the family bought a new television that received ITV as well as BBC programmes.

them were my relatives and some of them were friends but you'd knock on one door and say 'You coming out to play?' and everybody would be out. On bank holidays, I remember twenty of us walking as a group to Handsworth Park and playing football. The older kids would look out for the younger ones. When you walked to the park, there was people you knew. Everybody knew everybody. That's why you never played up! There was a large Sikh community but in my street there was Irish people, there was English people, there was no racial barriers. I remember growing up playing with white children, Sikh children, West Indian children. You never thought 'I am not playing with him because he is black – or white'.

Gurdip Gill, born 1969

A Nineties Childhood

When I was about six, in 1969/70, I used to go to bed on my own. I was never taken to bed. I never had to be told, I just went to bed. My bedroom door was shut although maybe there was a landing light on. There was no questions asked, I just went to bed. With my children now in 1999, it's such a rigmarole. They've got televisions in their bedroom and they've got videos. They must own, between them, 250 video films. For them to go to bed, they must have their television on. If they haven't got their television on, they can't go to sleep and if anything happens to their video, they expect you to be able to go and buy them another one.

Maria Finch, born 1963

Richard Jeffs, his mother and their dog, Tassie, 1959.

A Fifties Childhood

I was born after rationing was finished. I really was lucky because I missed rationing and I was growing up at a time when Britain was doing reasonably well. We didn't have everything, but I never knew what hunger was. Mum and dad and me lived in this three-bedroom semi in Collingdon Avenue in Sheldon, and my grandparents and my father's sister lived in Clements Road in Yardley. It was a really neat little family unit and I was spoilt rotten because I was an only child.

Richard Jeffs, born 1954

Educating Girls

In 1922, when I was fourteen, I would have liked to have gone on to a teacher training centre but my father thought it was a waste of time because I would be at least twenty-one before I would be earning and then I would probably be married and I wouldn't be able to teach. I suppose he didn't want to see me as a permanent maiden lady like a lot of the teachers were.

Gwendoline Webb, born 1908

Harry and Doris Phillips in the garden of Doris' parents' house in Springfield Avenue, Balsall Heath, 1941. They met when they both worked at H.E. Rudge in Emily Street.

Family Ties

I left school at fourteen and started to work the next day for 11s a week. That was at a brass founders, H.E. Rudge in Emily Street, working from eight o'clock in the morning to six o'clock at night, five days a week and Saturday until half past twelve. My father spoke for me, that's how you got jobs in those days. Nearly all my relations worked for H.E. Rudge at some time or other, including my own wife. That's where I met her.

Harry Phillips, born 1922

Following On

I got a job in 1965, with my dad and my brother, in Lucas' car component factory. I knew I was going to get in

there two years before because there was a family thing, you followed on. It was only a matter of time before I moved into Lucas. I already knew the foreman and I already knew most of the lads through listening to my dad talk about them.

Larry Finglass, born 1946

Delivering Bread

I helped a baker one time. This was in the days when bread was delivered on a horse and cart, and there was no such thing as sliced bread. You went to the baker and he owned the horses and the cart. You hired the cart from him and you bought the bread off him. Well, you could buy yesterday's bread cheaper. The guy I helped, bought half and half – half of yesterday's bread, half of today's fresh bread. When we set off, he used to put two loaves on the seat unwrapped and he said 'Sit on there, son' and I thought 'How nice of him'. So I sat on there. Then he'd say 'Right, jump off' and he'd pick up the two loaves, knock on the door and the woman would say 'Oh, these are lovely and fresh. They're still warm'.

Dan Jones, born 1929

Tram Blocks

Towards the end of the '30s, they started to rip up the tram lines and bring on petrol-driven buses. The tramlines were laid in wooden blocks and the oil leaking from the trams had soaked into these wooden blocks. I got the family pram and I asked them 'Could I have the wooden blocks?' I wheeled them into our back yard and chopped them into bundles of firewood. I went to the local hardware shop, Mr Ellwood, that used to sell firewood and I said 'Do you want to buy these bundles of firewood? They're soaked in oil, they'll burn wonderful'. So, I sold him quite a few bundles then I chopped some more bundles and I went round door-to-door selling them at the houses. Then the next week, I went to Mr Ellwood and I said 'Do you want some more?' and he said 'No, they don't seem to be going very well'. Well, of course, I was selling door-to-door to his customers so I was getting two bites of the cherry. Then the police came to school and said 'It has come to our notice that people are using these oil-

The passing out parade of the St John's Ambulance Brigade, Lucas', Sparkhill, 1967. Like many people, Larry Finglass joined a factory where his father was already working.

31

Dan Jones, aged eight in 1937, had a range of money making schemes.

there. You wouldn't even have to walk into a lesson and listen to a teacher to learn about the world, you could stand in the courtyard having a fag with someone and just learn all about different people's cultures, backgrounds and lives. I've been a year and a half through my course now and it's been the best part of my life.

Morgan, born 1981

soaked blocks for lighting fires and causing a lot of chimney fires'. They were getting word round that they were dangerous to use, but I had already made my fortune.

Dan Jones, born 1929

Sixth Form College

I remember walking into my interview at Joseph Chamberlain Sixth Form College and I must have been the only white kid in the room. I felt really threatened because I had never been the minority before and this was the first time. I just remember loving being

CHAPTER 2
Marriage and babies

Bob and Irene Houghton on their wedding day, 25 October 1958. The wedding breakfast included tea, cold meat and pork pies and was held in Irene's mother's front parlour.

Tearful Parting

During that year from 1940 to 1941, we had a very pleasant year. Almost twelve months to the day of my marriage, my husband was called up. He had always wanted to fly so he went into the airforce and hoped to be a pilot. That was a terrible parting, lots of tears, knowing that it would be more than likely that he wouldn't come back. It was a period of dread that our happiness was going to end because of the war.

Renee Kingston, born 1918

Courting

When we was courting, even when we was engaged, if I was saying goodnight to my wife in their entry, say at half nine, ten o'clock, her mother used to be on the doorstep shouting 'Ain't you coming in tonight?' That was ten o'clock at night and she was eighteen.

Harry Phillips, born 1922

Bottom Drawer

I used to house my bottom drawer in a tea chest and I used to love to get it out every now and then to examine what I'd got for my future home. A bottom drawer was our goods to help us to set up home. Chiefly they were little items of linen, also china, so that when I started my home, I had a good start in life.

Renee Kingston, born 1918

Arthur Hickerton (standing, on the right) joined the RAF as a navigator. He was killed in Northern Greece during the Second World War.

A Sister's Opinion

In Islamic culture and law we are allowed to marry first cousins. They look round in the family to see who is eligible and who is compatible for each other. So my cousin is my husband now. They saw that he's educated, he's from Pakistan and he's sort of the right age. My sister and my older sister actually said to me 'God, Neila he's really nice for you to marry' and I just said 'What you talking about Guzala, I'm not interested. Don't be stupid' and she was like 'No, no he's really nice'. She went to his house. He made them tea. He fried fresh samosas. He did it like a girl basically. Men don't do that or you don't see that very often, and she said she was so surprised and she really likes him for me.

Neila Butt, born 1970

Wendy Fenn aged nineteen with her fiancé Derek, Church Road, Sheldon, in 1960.

Honeymoon

We had our honeymoon at Butlin's in Scarborough in 1948 with two kids. My wife hadn't seen the sea until then. In those days, if you had a holiday, you would go to Sutton Coldfield or Lickey Hills.

Harry Phillips, born 1922

Kissing in the Street

I was about eighteen and we were standing at the bus stop and he kissed me goodbye. Kissing in the street in the '50s and '60s was taboo and one of my neighbours who was very nosy, happened to be in his garden behind his big thistle. He went and told my mother. He said 'It's disgraceful, I saw your daughter kissing her boyfriend at the bus stop'. My mother said 'What is it to do with you?' So really in those days, she was enlightened.

Wendy Fenn, born 1942

Rush to Marry

Charles and I got engaged on 24 May 1939 and of course on 3 September 1939, war was declared. There was an awful rush for people to get married, principally because if the man went

Marjorie and Charles Sanders were married on 30 September 1939.

away to war, there would be a marriage allowance. My fiancé was a wood pattern maker so although he was of call-up age, he was not accepted because of his trade. In spite of that we decided to get married on 30 September 1939. We got married at the Registry Office in Birmingham and on that day people were literally standing in queues to get married. I didn't like that so we had a special licence which enabled us to have a nice private room and a little ceremony.

Marjorie Sanders, born 1915

Engaged

We had the engagement on the phone. I was at work and they said to me 'Oh, there's a phone call for you from home'. My mum said 'Well, they've got you engaged'. My uncle had actually gone over to Pakistan, got it all sorted out and got the ring. It sounds so strange to a Western culture. I said 'Oh my God

mum. Are you sure?' and she said 'Well, yeah, it's done now'. I'd only met him briefly when I went on my visit a year or so before.

Neila Butt, born 1970

Bridesmaids' Dresses

In 1947, clothing coupons were still in use. I was able to buy a second-hand wedding dress. I wanted two bridesmaids and I went to Rackhams every day for a fortnight. One day they'd had three bolts of crepe material in and I dashed up and put my hand on one and said 'I want 12 yards of that one please for the bridesmaids' dresses'. The reception was at an inn and the lady asked if mother could get a ham and a tongue because otherwise she would find it very difficult to provide the meal for us.

Joan Stoker, born 1922

Marriage Today

I am thirty-five, my husband is thirty-nine. We both feel that we are probably in a minority when it comes to being married. A lot of our children's friends' parents aren't married. They have either been married and got divorced or they have never been married, they just live together. I don't disagree with it.

Maria Finch, born 1963

Living Together

I met my current partner in 1987 so I was seventeen at the time. I met him at a party, he was a friend of a friend, and I have been with him ever since. I think my parents find it hard to believe that I've been with the same person for twelve years. I think we've grown up together. We've been through incredibly hard patches where we've thought that we might finish. A lot of my friends of my age, twenty-eight, some of them have been married and divorced. Some of my friends are married but are going through a difficult patch. Some of them have had loads and loads of partners. Some of them get very bitter and twisted and cynical. I am very lucky not to have that. I currently live with my boyfriend. It doesn't bother me living with him before getting married. When I first moved in with my boyfriend, my nan was still alive and she was an incredibly strict Catholic. I wondered how I was going to tackle it with her because I couldn't tell her that I was living with my boyfriend.

Emma Richardson, born 1970

Marriage before Children

If I wanted children, I would like to be married first. I suppose that's a strange mixture of thoughts. I think a lot of my friends that are the same age as me, think exactly the same. They think 'It's fine to live together before you are married, no problem at all but if we are going to have children, I think it has to be a bit more permanent than that'. I think I'd like to be married. I think I'd like to be a Mrs. I think there is still a slight stigma attached if you are a single parent. I don't think that's right at all. If I got pregnant tomorrow, I would have the child but I would prefer to be married.

Emma Richardson, born 1970

Emma Richardson and her fiancé, Craig Clarke, at a friend's wedding, July 1998.

Supportive Wife

I got married in 1966. My wife came over from Pakistan. She is my first cousin and I had known her from childhood. We were engaged when I came here and I said 'I'll come back in a couple of years and get married'. But that never happened. I invited her here and we got married and I started a business. She was very supportive and used to look after the shop. She is an educated girl and could cope. Most of the women who came from Pakistan didn't want to mix with men but she came from an enlightened family so she didn't mind.

Mohammed Ayyub, born 1939

Choosing a Wife

I married a second generation Greek Cypriot girl born in London because it was my choice to do that – nothing to do with 'English aren't good enough'. Marriage is a partnership and if you've got a mixed culture when you go through a bad patch, this could start causing a few problems in the marriage. I saw it as a duty to my roots to marry my own type and to carry on the tradition and for both of us to be happy. I've got to accept that there's a 90% chance that my children are going to marry English but if I don't want that to happen I should go to Cyprus. We'll go to a Greek wedding and I'll have friends there who have married English people and you won't be able to speak Greek, you have to speak

Harry and Doris Phillips were married at St Paul's church, Moseley Road, Balsall Heath in 1944. Harry was allowed thirty-six hours leave from the RAF to get married.

A wedding card sent to Harry and Doris Phillips by relatives in Canada.

English. And they feel embarrassed that you are having to speak English to make them feel comfortable.

Gabriel Gabriel, born 1963

Married Life

About a year and a half after we were engaged, I went to Pakistan and we got married. Now two and a half years later, I have a baby boy. He's wonderful. My husband is now over here with a legal visa to work and it couldn't be better. I knew from the first month I was with him in Pakistan that I'd made the right decision. I'm happy and contented. I know I can spend the rest of my life with this man.

Neila Butt, born 1970

One Night of Love

I came home in 1946 and me and the wife were waiting to get married. At that time I was on combined operations and we kept getting our leave stopped. Eventually we did get married on a thirty-six hour pass which meant I'd got to come from the other side of London up to Birmingham, get married and go back. I left the unit at four o'clock in the afternoon, got to New Street at eleven o'clock at night. I had to walk all the way to Small Heath and there was an air raid on at the time. We got married at half past two on the Saturday and on the Sunday at twelve o'clock, I was on the train back to the unit. So it was one night of love. That's what they sang to the wife when she walked into the office the next day.

Harry Phillips, born 1922

Marriages

I've got four brothers, three of whom are married. One of them is married to a Sikh girl and two of them have got white wives but they are all accepted. My father, I think, deep down possibly he wanted his sons to marry into a Sikh family but he has always said 'As long as my sons are happy, I'm happy'. He dotes on his grandchildren and there is no difference between the grandchildren if they are mixed race or not, he treats them all the same.

Gurdip Gill, born 1969

Arranged Marriage

I said to my dad 'It's time for me to get married'. He said 'Son, leave it to me. I'm going to spread it round the people from my village who live in England. We'll get a nice girl from around our villages'. A few weeks later, he gets a call from the middle man – he knows me and he knows the girl and he obviously has some judge of character. So they arranged an initial meeting and there was the middle man, his wife, his daughter, my dad and then there was me at the end of the row of people. We went out for a coffee at a café but there was no

Gurmej Gill and his grandsons, Jashaan and Raajan. (Courtesy of Olan Mills)

direct conversation between me and Mary, my wife. We came back to Birmingham. Then Mary's dad phoned the middle man to say that she said 'yes' and that we should proceed to the next stage. So we went out together and I said 'We've got to be honest with each other, if we decide to carry on and date, we've got to give it 100%'. I was trying to put a few obstacles in her way so if she did say yes, she was sure. She said 'Yes'. I didn't know what to do, I was embarrassed. I didn't even kiss her on the cheek to say goodbye, I was in shock. So we dated and then we decided to get engaged.

Gabriel Gabriel, born 1963

A New Marriage

I was a single parent for many, many years although my son did have regular contact with his father and there were other adults around helping but I recently got married. I never thought I'd end up with a Caribbean man because their ways of thinking, their tastes, their ways of life are different to black British men and I was always a bit intimidated by them. You have to be able to cook in a certain way, you have to bring up your children in a certain way and you have to think a certain way, but it's new and I'm enjoying learning. Sometimes I get it wrong and he gets a bit frustrated with me but most of the time, he's very kind, very gentle and very patient.

Malika Ahmed, born 1967

Malika Ahmed and her son, Lucian, outside the Seventh Day Adventist church, Birmingham, 1987.

Choosing a Husband

When I get married, the race of my husband wouldn't matter to me because I would take them for who they are, what their personality is like, if they are loving and caring. Race doesn't matter at all. My parents don't want me to have an arranged marriage, and I don't want to have an arranged marriage either. My mother didn't have one. I suppose I'll get married when I want and to who I want. It depends when I am ready.

Lara Coles, born 1983

English Boyfriend

I have an English boyfriend and I met him at a party. We hit it off from day one. I have been involved with other people but this is my first serious relationship. My dad, I know, wants me to find this fine Irish lad. I remember feeling that was what my dad wanted from me. I think they probably are slightly disappointed that my boyfriend is of English background but that is made up for by the fact that he is such a nice lad and that they do really like him. To me, it makes no difference at all whether he is English or Irish.

Martha McCarron, born 1972

Bonding

I was twenty-four and my parents were keen to have me settled. They said to me 'Right Affie, we've found someone for you'. The day I went to see Satvinder, I didn't think too much about it because I was too preoccupied with a trip to Scotland for a possible job. We went to the middle man's house. I wasn't particularly bothered what Satvinder looked like, as long as they were a good family. I think the whole meeting must have taken half an hour. Me and Satvinder went to a separate room and had a quick chat about what we wanted from life. I said 'We need to be completely honest about what you want from marriage and what I want'. I said to him 'How would you feel if I didn't come home until the middle of the night because I was too busy working?' He said 'Life is a compromise'. And that bonded us together.

Avtar Tulwar, born 1969

Avtar Tulwar on her wedding day, walking down a corridor in the temple, accompanied by her brothers and sister, 1993.

Avtar and Satvinder's official wedding photograph, 1993. (Courtesy of Olan Mills)

Gurdip and Janjeet Gill. (Courtesy of Olan Mills)

Registry Office Wedding

It was quite a big affair, my Registry Office wedding, because we had a huge party afterwards which was not normal because you have a huge party after the Indian wedding. A lot of people in the community don't recognise the Registry wedding as an official wedding. I had a vintage car and I had a beautiful ivory silk wedding dress. My nieces were my bridesmaids. We did not live together afterwards. It is not recognised within the Asian community. You are only married when you have your religious wedding which is a year after. We didn't court until after the civil wedding. A year later we had our religious wedding and I didn't enjoy that at all. The bride is meant to

be quiet and submissive. Not a lot of people understand what is going on. It is quite a hectic, draining day. In the evening you go back to your in-laws' house. It's the strangest feeling being in someone else's house that you are meant to call home and to be married to this man that you don't really know that well.

Avtar Tulwar, born 1969

Decision to Marry

In 1989, I met Janjeet at a place in the centre of town where I was working. It started off as a friendship and it progressed on to a relationship. People class it as a love marriage. I told my dad and the first thing he asked me is 'What village is she from?' Being from the Punjab, everybody knows everybody. She told her parents and it was accepted. Once we'd announced that we wanted to get married, I did feel a bit of pressure that it should happen there and then. An Asian wedding is an experience in itself and I've got to admit, I didn't enjoy it. A lot of people thought the marriage wouldn't work because it was a love marriage, but we are still going strong.

Gurdip Gill, born 1969

Catholic Attitudes

It is more acceptable for the young Catholic generation to be involved in a sexual relationship but I still think that they don't enter it as lightly. They are still very conscious of making that decision. Then there is the Catholic guilt because you could be involved in a sexual relationship but it clashes with your religious beliefs. It is hard really to gel the two. It is becoming more acceptable really for young people to have sex before they get married. Young people feel that the consequence of getting divorced is far worse than actually becoming sexually involved with somebody and it not working out. If you get divorced, you stay single for the rest of your life or else you're going to be committing adultery. There is no getting through the gates of heaven if you are committing adultery. I've had a young friend who is in that situation, she is riddled with guilt. One time, she was saying to me 'I am going to Hell because of what I have done'.

Martha McCarron, born 1972

Dowry

Me dad said 'Come and join me at work because we've got to generate a bit of a dowry, to accumulate some money to help marry your sisters off'. Any parent when their child gets married, if they can afford a little bit extra, provides them with furniture for the house, it's every parent's duty. It was a duty and a Greek Cypriot tradition to provide a dowry for the daughters, a tradition that was still being carried on in the 1980s in Britain. We made this dowry for my sisters. They all got married and they had their furniture or a contribution to a deposit on their house. They were gently weaned into their married life with fewer financial difficulties.

Gabriel Gabriel, born 1963

Husband's Death

In 1943, I had become pregnant and we were thrilled to bits because we had been married three and a half years and I was approaching twenty-five. My mother wanted me back home with her so that when I had the baby I would

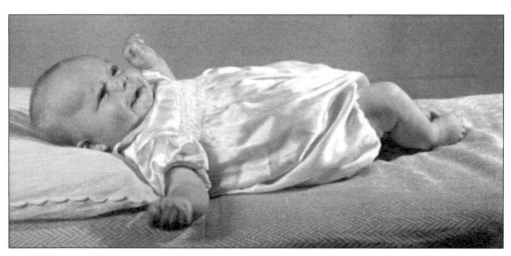

John Hickerton aged two months, 1944. His mother, Renee, was widowed just before John was born.

have some support. I was in bed one day and my mother came up to my bedroom and said 'Renee, a funny telegram has arrived for you'. Straight away I just knew that it was a telegram to say that my husband Arthur was either missing or had been killed. Sure enough it was to say that they were missing from air operations. So there I was seven months pregnant and so happy with my husband, a lovely, charming, good looking man and thinking 'What on earth is going to happen to me?' Then in January 1944, I had the letter to say that the crew had been presumed to have been killed in Northern Greece. And then John was born. I was a fortnight with false labour. I kept on starting and stopping. I think it was probably due to shock. He arrived on 26 January 1944.

Renee Kingston, born 1918

Illegitimacy

I remember one night, two of us midwives were not very busy and we decided to see how many patients had 'had to get married', had shot gun weddings. The hospital had something like forty to fifty patients and we counted up the hospital register and a quarter of those mums had had to get married while they were pregnant. This was in 1936. When I think back to those days, there was far more girls getting married while they were pregnant than people realise. Some of them in sheer ignorance. I know maids were often accosted by the master or the elder son of the house and had no choice. If people think that there were no single mums in the mid-'30s, I could

tell them different. It was really very sad.

Ellen O'Brien, born 1911

Condoms

When we was kids, you didn't get free condoms. You used to have to get your condoms from the barber's or the chemist's shop and pay half a crown for three. When you used to go to the chemist shop, there'd be a woman serving or there were people there. All the condoms were not on show, they were hidden away under the counter. For a girl to a have a baby in those days, it was a crime if she wasn't married.

Harry Phillips, born 1922

Married in White

It was a terrible disgrace if you had a baby at a young age. The girl next door to us got into trouble and she got married. My mother was laughing and said that the neighbours had been talking – 'Fancy having a wedding like that, and in white. She's not pure, she's no right to wear white'.

Gwendoline Webb, born 1908

A Woman's Responsibility

My mother is eighty-nine and she says now 'None of my girls brought trouble to my doorstep'. It was instilled into us that as the girl you took responsibility and you'd say 'No, that's enough'. In 1959/60, it was still a disgrace to be an unmarried mother. I did have friends who got to nineteen, twenty and had a child but usually it was adopted. It wasn't kept within the family. I had one friend and her baby was adopted. You didn't keep them because of the stigma. A lot of young women really suffered because they had to give their child up. I don't think boys and men have ever taken full responsibility for sex, it's always been on the shoulders of the woman. It was your responsibility. They were never blamed. For women, you were either a fast woman or you were virtuous.

Norma Morgan, born 1937

Respectability

Working class people were very keen to be respectable. There were two things you must never do when I was growing up – you mustn't have a baby before you were married and you mustn't get into debt.

Joan Stoker, born 1922

Baby on the Way

I was so naïve, I didn't even know I was pregnant after I got married. My mother said to me, 'Do you think you could be pregnant?' I'd been married three months and I just looked at her and said 'No'. She said 'Well, you are married aren't you? I think you'd better go to the doctor'.

Wendy Fenn, born 1942

Pregnancy before Marriage

My mother was pregnant before she got married which was a terrible thing for her family. That was 1921. Her older sister, who was climbing the ladder a bit at Cadbury's, refused to be bridesmaid but she came to the wedding. It was quite obvious that she didn't approve. My mother and father didn't tell us that was the situation. One day, we were looking in the family Bible where the dates of marriage and birth of our parents had been recorded. When we discovered this, my mother was terribly upset when she realised we knew. We just had to accept it. When their silver wedding came along, it was rather difficult to make an occasion of it

Wendy Fenn with her new baby, Debbie, and her parents-in-law, Tower Road, Aston, 1962.

Joan Stoker's parents, Olive Powell and Percy Harper, were married on 26 December 1921. Olive was already expecting their first child.

Lorna Hancox, her son, Andrew and brother, David, 1990.

because I was nearly twenty-five myself at the time.

Joan Stoker, born 1922

Changes for Single Parents

I think it's very different today. My mother was a single parent because of divorce but she had been married. My daughter had not been married when she had her son at nineteen. Nobody seemed to be too worried about it from the stigmatising point of view, apart from me and her father. As the child of divorced parents in the 1940s and '50s, there was definitely a stigma almost as bad as being illegitimate. Today, in the main, being a single parent is a choice, with contraception being what it is. In the 1940s, there wasn't the choice, you were pregnant and that was it.

Rita Hancox, born 1937

Resisting Peer Pressure

When I was seventeen or eighteen, when my friends were becoming sexually involved, you daren't do it because there was pressure at home. It was ingrained at home from an early age. The consequence of being pregnant, the scandal and everybody back in Ireland knowing that you got pregnant, that's the best contraceptive going. It was more than enough of a deterrent.

Martha McCarron, born 1972

Too Many Children

I don't believe society recognises the importance of the contraceptive, now girls can plan their families. I can remember in 1957 when I was working as a midwife, I had a young woman who was not yet thirty and I went to her for her ninth baby. I reckon from the moment she was married to then, she had only had the first nine months of her marriage when she was neither breastfeeding or having a baby. Her varicose veins were dreadful. She was about twenty-nine years old so I suggested to her that she went to the family planning and she said she'd go. To my horror, the next year, I attended her again. When it was all over, I said to her 'Why the tenth baby? What happened to family planning?' She told me she was a Roman Catholic and that the priest and her husband got hold of the idea that she was going and made her life so miserable that they made sure she didn't go. So she said 'This time I went without them knowing. When the priest found out, he came and gave me a lecture. When he finished, I said "Right, I'll go out and you come in. You get the dinner ready for twelve of them and see how you feel at the end of it and then we'll talk"'.

Ellen O'Brien, born 1911

Having His Pleasure

I remember back in the '30s, I was in a house where there was a charlady and I used to talk to her quite a lot. She had ten children and she used to talk to me about them. I said 'Why have ten? Why not say no?' She said 'You don't know what you are talking about, nurse. He comes home in the dinner hour and wants his bit of pleasure'. I was shocked. I said 'What would happen if you said no?' She said 'He'd stick me head in the copper if it

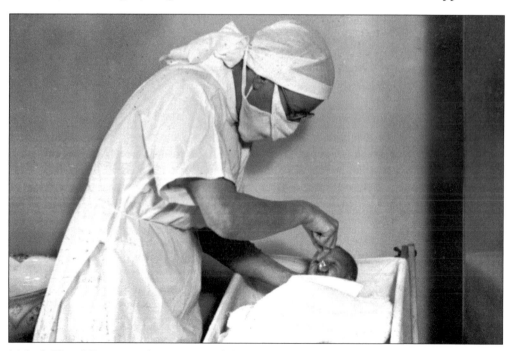

Midwife Ellen O'Brien cares for a premature baby in a patient's home. She is shown giving the baby some medicine.

was on'. She said 'Monday morning, you see people with black eyes, what do you think it is a result of?'

Ellen O'Brien, born 1911

Single Parent

My husband having been killed in the war in late 1943, I was a single parent. I don't recall a lot of my friends were in the same position, it was quite unusual. In our neighbourhood they were all very, very sorry for me. A chemist who lived nearby in Balsall Heath, he and his wife had no children and they used to take John out in the pram for walks and wondered if they could adopt him. I think they anticipated that a single parent couldn't possibly be able to bring up a child on their own.

Renee Kingston, born 1918

Divorce

On the anniversary of our wedding, I found a note on my dressing table, telling me that my husband was leaving me. In 1962, I divorced him. Divorce in those days was a bit different from today. I remember a colleague coming to me and saying 'It's so humiliating for a woman isn't it?' One of the biggest difficulties was that you could do nothing on your own. If I'd wanted to buy a house, I would have had to get his permission, even though he was my ex-husband. A woman on her own, divorced or single, had to have a man to stand security for

Renee Hickerton (now Kingston) and her son John in 1946. Renee was widowed at the age of twenty-five in 1943, just before John was born.

her loan, whether it was for a gramophone or a house.

Ellen O'Brien, born 1911

Parents' Divorce

My parents had divorced and at school the emphasis on family life was quite important. I felt quite intimidated by this fact because even though I was completely happy living with my father, it was completely different to all my friends at school where they had a mother and a father. My mother lived in London and even though I had her support, it wasn't in

Bob Houghton, his brother John and mother Polly, 1940. During the Second World War, Polly worked as a clippie (conductor) on Birmingham buses.

everyday life so we had to make a lot of effort to make it work out. This made me feel quite withdrawn.

Katherine O'Donnell, born 1977

An Abused Mother

At the age of six, I knew that my mum was a battered wife. I've actually seen my dad punch my mum with his fist. I remember once jumping on his back trying to save my mum and he flung me somehow and I ended up against the wall. He actually punched me with one fist and blacked both my eyes.

Bob Houghton, born 1936

Police Called

I remember my mum getting dad some chops. He came home drunk and he threw the chop and the dinner up the wall. He upped the table and smashed windows. And the police came to our house and the policeman said to our mum 'Call us in missus and we'll do him'. She said 'I daren't, I can't'. My mum still wouldn't say anything against him. When he used to hit us, she always used to get hysterical. She would go for my dad then but she would always end up the loser. She would have nothing said against him. My sister is fifty now and the day she was born, was the day dad decided to leave mum for this other woman. The day she was born.

Bob Houghton, born 1936

Parents' Divorce

We came back from holiday and my father had decided that he was going to leave and live with the woman that he had been having a relationship with. It was devastating. My mother was totally devastated because he had been her childhood sweetheart. My mother was crying. They actually divorced in 1949. Divorce is something nobody in the family had ever done. My father's parents were totally horrified. It was so hard, people didn't get divorced. I could never tell anybody that my parents were divorced, I never did. When I was at school I never discussed it. I used to say my dad was away working. I used to be absolutely terrified that I would come home and find that my mum had gone. Dad had gone, was mum going to go as well?

Rita Hancox, born 1937

Going Out

Being a Sikh and being a teenager in 1985/86, there wasn't much sex

Rita Abbott (now Hancox) with her parents Phyllis and Charles on their last family holiday in Weymouth, before her parents' divorce, 1948.

education in the home so a lot of what you learnt was from your peers. At school it was a bit of a taboo subject. As an Asian Sikh man, it was acceptable for me to go out in the evening but for a young teenage girl of my age it would have been very difficult. In 1999, there is equality now with Asian women.

Gurdip Gill, born 1969

Women's Role

When I was a young woman, especially from a working class background, you got to nineteen or twenty, you were married and you had children. I accepted that. As the wife, you did all the cooking, cleaning and the keeping of the house. The time you spent in the house with the children had no value because you hadn't been to work all day. In the past, once you were married, you were married and you stayed in that marriage. I was thirty when I first saw the light and I realised that everything I did had been determined for me. Men had made all these decisions.

Norma Morgan, born 1937

Domestic Roles

People have a perception of an Asian marriage, of the man being very chauvinist and the woman doing the cooking and the cleaning and looking after the kids but it's not like that now. In the old days, it was the man who went out to work and the woman stayed at home but now in the '90s, it's reliant on both parents going to work. We share everything. I was there for the birth of our children and every step of the way through the pregnancy I went to the appointments with Janjeet. Even though I am a Sikh, I am my own person. I am a Sikh but I don't lead my life according to what tradition says, I follow my course as I want to – changing nappies, cooking and cleaning, I think we do 50/50.

Gurdip Gill, born 1969

Mums and Dads

At school its not just mums in the playground, there are a lot of dads. Some of them work at Rover at Longbridge and they do shifts so they take their turn to bring the kids into school. There's other dads who do role reversal. There's other men who are married to childminders and they do childminding as well.

Maria Finch, born 1963

CHAPTER 3

Making ends meet

Demolition of Birmingham's slum houses went on until the 1960s. Over the years conditions had been growing steadily worse. The overcrowding and poverty that many people lived with are hard to imagine today.

Pawning a Bundle

Women would get up at about five o'clock in the morning and do their washing, hang it out and it would be dry enough to bring into pawn. They would pawn a bundle of a shirt, a tablecloth, a blouse and a sheet and my mother would perhaps lend 4s 6d on that bundle. If it was a larger one, 6s 6d or 8s 6d. The charge was according to where they wanted it hung. If they wanted it in the drawer, it would perhaps be an extra 2d but if they wanted it on a hanger it would be 3d. They could leave the bundle in for a week or a fortnight or even a month. They could leave it in for twelve months and we'd got to look after that bundle for twelve months. At the end of twelve months, we were allowed to sell anything because it became our property.

Renee Kingston, born 1918

Working in the Shop

My mother was in charge of the shop. When we first had the shop, we were only doing a very few pledges a week. My mother built up the shop until we were taking in 800 items per week. As children, we used to come home from school, go straight into the shop, stand at the desk and enter the items. Each ticket had a counterfoil and the counterfoil went on the article of clothing or bundle and the corresponding number would be entered in a huge leather-bound book.

Renee Kingston, born 1918

The Tallyman

Well into the '50s, because money was still hard to get and mum had no husband to back her, she had to rely very heavily on pawn shops and the tallyman. Now, the tallyman was the devil in disguise. He would knock on the door and he would sell you shirts, shoes and loan you money. There was the 20 shilling chance. You would buy the chance and they would always charge you 21 or 22 shillings for the chance. He would sell a £2 shirt for 2 shillings a week and mum would have these shirts off him but she used to take them to the pawn shop – we never wore them. The pawn shop was our salvation. I'd always got to go down to my 'Auntie Alice' with this bundle. I always thought she was a relation. The lady that ran the pawn shop, we used to call our Auntie Alice and I genuinely believed that we was related and that she was my auntie. I used to take this bundle down and take the money back to my mum.

Bob Houghton, born 1936

Paying the Butcher

We used to have money owing to our butcher's shop. Everything was on tick. Nobody ever paid. They used to say 'Charge it!' We never got it. The tallyman used to come round selling things. You'd have a pair of blankets and you'd pay a shilling a week. He used to come round and collect it and before you were half way through that, he used to sell you something else so in the end you owed

Ormond Street, 1904.

more than you could afford.

Stanley Webb, born 1916

Provident Cheques

There was never any cash.
Everything was hire purchase and as
soon as you paid off one thing, you'd
have something else. I was clothed on
Provident Cheques and when the
cheque had been paid for, I'd have
another new set of clothes. There was a
company called the Provident Clothing
Company. You'd have a cheque and
you'd pay this back at 2s a week and the
Provident man used to come round
every week and collect the money.
When it was paid for, he'd give you

another cheque. It was never ending.
Once you got into that trap with the
Provident Cheques, you never got out of
it, you was always in debt. My family
bought everything, even the clothes on
our back, on hire purchase. There was a
sign on a shop window and it said
'Provident Cheques accepted'. A lot of
people used to get furniture on this hire
purchase system and the next week,
they'd sell it.

George Turner, born 1932

Borrowing a Shilling

In the 1930s, there was more of a sense
of community. We were in and out of
each other's houses. Everybody knew

Price Street, 1904.

everybody's business and everybody knew what everybody else had got. People would borrow 6d off a neighbour one week and they'd borrow it back the next week. Nobody paid immediately for the things they had, it was on tick. You would try and charm the shopkeeper into letting you have things with the promise that you'd try and pay later on. A lot of people didn't of course. The children were sent to borrow the money, the parents never went themselves. They thought they stood a better chance of borrowing from neighbours if they sent the children round. I can remember being sent round to borrow a shilling off a friend of my father and of course, his immediate response was 'When am I going to get back the one he had last week?'

Ray Pegg, born 1928

The Pop Shop

We had nice customers who had big families and who were in dire straits. One woman would arrive in a taxi, the taxi being left along the road so that it wouldn't cause her any embarrassment. This particular woman lived in Edgbaston. There was one instance when she came at about eight o'clock at night and in a terrible state of distress because her husband wanted his suit because there was £20 in the waistcoat pocket. The woman was in a terrible state, she'd pretended to her husband that it was at the cleaners whereas in fact it was at the pop shop.

Renee Kingston, born 1918

58

Pawning the Iron

We had another woman who was a boozer. Practically every Wednesday she would come in. She was a huge woman with a great big white apron on. She would want to pawn the flat iron, upon which we lent 8d, to enable her to buy a pint of beer.

Renee Kingston, born 1918

Aston Slums

In 1941, when I was thirty, I found myself working as a midwife in the slums of Aston. It was indescribable. I was really shocked at these back-to-back houses. I left the slums in 1944 and in those years, I'd learned to respect the women tremendously. The average number of children was six, but quite a lot of those mothers had eight, nine, ten, or even as many as twelve. No hot water in the house, some of them no water at all in the house, no inside toilets of any sort.

Ellen O'Brien, born 1911

Cockroaches

We were moved out of back-to-backs in Hope Street in Balsall Heath in 1966, to Lincoln Street where the houses were slightly more modern. They then conducted a programme of slum clearance including Hope Street School. They were rat, mice and cockroach infested. We used to have a cellar where the coal man used to come and he'd take the grating off the cellar

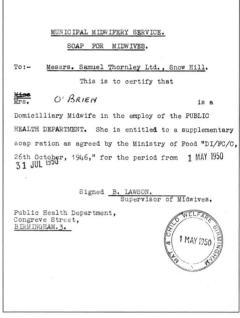

MUNICIPAL MIDWIFERY SERVICE.

SOAP FOR MIDWIVES.

To:- Messrs. Samuel Thornley Ltd., Snow Hill.

This is to certify that

~~Miss~~ Mrs. O'BRIEN is a Domicilliary Midwife in the employ of the PUBLIC HEALTH DEPARTMENT. She is entitled to a supplementary soap ration as agreed by the Ministry of Food "DI/FC/C, 26th October, 1946," for the period from 1 MAY 1950 31 JUL 1950

Signed B. LAWSON.
Supervisor of Midwives.

Public Health Department,
Congreve Street,
BIRMINGHAM. 3.

1 MAY 1950

A certificate issued to Ellen O'Brien allowing her extra soap rations for her work as a midwife.

and throw down sacks of coal. When we wanted coal for the fire, we used to have to use the internal steps to the cellar. We'd go down those steps hearing the crunch of cockroaches under foot making an awful cracking noise. We'd shovel a bucket of coal and bring it up for mum or dad to put on the fire. Dad used to set mouse traps everywhere.

Steve Rogers, born 1957

Overcrowding

There were some houses that were really, really dirty. I remember on one occasion, I was called into a place in Aston. I was going up the stairs and I stepped over a bundle. And remember that in 1942, we had blackout and there was no gas either, but we had candles. I was sitting on the bed at about three o'clock in the morning, looking at the wall and suddenly I thought 'That wall is moving'. So I took a candle, went up to it and it was moving. It was alive. I don't know what insect it was, but it was alive. When I went down the stairs again, the bundle that I thought was just a bundle of clothes was in actual fact a child sleeping on the stairs. There were twelve children in that little two up, two down. She had given up, that particular woman. I don't think she'd combed her hair or washed or anything. There was a smell in those houses and I think it was the smell of bugs. But they were the exception, they really were.

Ellen O'Brien, born 1911

Kent Street Baths

In Milk Street, they were real back-to-back houses, real slums. Moving from there to Northfield, it was much better. The houses were semi-detached. It was luxury but there was still no hot water in the houses. We had a cold water system but to us that was a luxury

Washing a baby in the public baths. Going to the baths was the only way that most people in the inner city had access to hot running water.

60

having come from Milk Street. In Northfield, we had a bathroom. Well, in Milk Street, there were no bathrooms so unless we did it in the kitchen in a zinc bath, we were taken to the baths and that's where everybody went. The baths were in Kent Street. You had to sit in a queue outside first and then you were taken to the bath. You had one big tap and the attendant used to have a big key and they'd fill the bath for you and you'd try the water and if it was too hot you'd say 'A bit more cold' or if it was too cold, you'd have a bit more hot. You were allowed twenty minutes and if you stayed in the bath more than twenty minutes, there'd be a banging on the door and you had to get out. They used to supply towels there but they were the size of a child's nappy so you always used to take your own towel.

George Turner, born 1932

Bugs

We had a plague of bugs. When you squash one, it leaves a red mark. You could always tell a house that has bugs because when you go in the door, it's got an acidy smell and you could smell them in the house. I used to lie on my bed as a child with a broom handle with a washer on the end and I used to be squashing the bugs on the ceiling because if they drop on you, they can bite so you can be eaten alive. My father used to build a fire up until in the end it was 100 degrees in the living room. The bugs couldn't stand heat so they would go right through the walls into next door and then they had a plague of bugs. It used to clear the house

CITY OF   BIRMINGHAM.

CORPORATION BATHS.

NOTICE.

THE

CORPORATION COTTAGE BATHS

SITUATED IN

COVENTRY STREET, off DIGBETH
BREARLEY STREET, off NEWTOWN ROW,
BACCHUS ROAD, off LODGE ROAD (WINSON GREEN),
AND
LOWER DARTMOUTH STREET (WHEN COMPLETED).

Will be open between the **1st** of **April** and the **30th September,** from **7 a.m.** until **9 p.m.,** and on Sunday Mornings **from 6 a.m.** until **11 o'clock a.m.** Admission until **8-30** on weekdays, and on Sunday Mornings **until 10 o'clock.**

From **October 1st** until **March 31st** the **Establishments** will be open from **8 a.m.** until **7 p.m.** on **Mondays, Tuesdays, Wednesdays,** and **Thursdays,** on **Fridays** until **8 o'clock,** and on **Saturdays** until **9 p.m.** throughout the year.

N.B.—The **Office is closed** 30 **minutes** earlier.

CHARGE FOR ADMISSION—
MEN or WOMEN, for a private hot or cold water bath, with the use of one towel - - - - - ONE PENNY.
SMALL SOAP TABLETS CAN BE PURCHASED AT THE OFFICE IF DESIRED AT AN EXTRA CHARGE OF · · ONE HALFPENNY.

Office, Kent Street,
April 1st, 1914.

[E.12566]

Pamphlet advertising the facilities at the washing baths in Coventry Street in 1914. Towels and soap cost extra.

for about six months, until next door decided to do the same and drove them back again.

Alfred Palmerfield, born 1927

Creepy Crawlies

Anything that used to crawl used to be in the house. The house had got no electric, just gas. When you lit the gas mantle when you came in, you could see all the floor had black-backs on it and they'd all disappear back off under the fire grate. You had a lot of livestock in the house that you didn't really want.

Alfred Palmerfield, born 1927

Housing Officer

We applied to Birmingham City Council for a house. The person who was responsible for allocating the houses was coming to see us, to see what accommodation we were living in. So I went and told my wife and we decided to move into the back bedroom – me, my wife and my young son. The Housing Officer came in and we went upstairs and we took her into the bedroom where there was just a double bed and a chest of drawers. She said 'Where does the baby sleep?' We said 'He has to sleep in bed with us'. 'My God' she said 'Can't you put him in one of the drawers and leave the drawer open?' 'Of course we can't, if we open the drawer, how can we get round the bed?' we said.

Alfred Bell, born 1919

Baths

There were washing baths, where for 6d you could go in and have a bath. There were all these cubicles in a row with baths and you went in and you paid your money. You took your own towel or you hired a towel for 2d. It only had one tap which was a cold tap. The other tap, you had to have a key for and you were allowed a certain ration of water for your 6d and you went in and you added your own cold water to suit. When I started work in the factories, it wasn't long before I found out how to make a key. So off I went to the baths, I paid my 6d, he give me my ration of hot water and went off. Then out of my pocket came the key and I started to add more water. What I didn't realise was that this water was measured

on a meter in his cubicle and he shouted 'Who's got the hot water on!'

Dan Jones, born 1929

Mail Boots

I didn't recognise it as poverty but obviously we were. I can remember every year, we had a card come through and mum used to take us up to town and we used to queue for these Daily Mail boots. They used to chafe you. They were the biggest things you'd ever saw. My brother would never go, he was a very proud lad. We had jerseys, we had trousers, we had socks and these boots. Everybody knew the Daily Mail boots, you could spot them a mile off. When we were at school in the playground, they used to chant 'Daily Mail boots', walking along behind you. They were enormous things. It was impossible to fall over, they were that big. To me they were fantastic, it didn't bother me what they shouted.

Dan Jones, born 1929

Big Feet

I've always had big feet. When we had clothing coupons, my mum always sold them because she couldn't afford boots for me. She sold the sweet coupons, not for her own gain but to buy a bit of food. There was the boot fund that gave a pair of boots to poor families at Christmas. So she went to the Birmingham Mail for this pair of boots, and she asked for a pair of size nines. They thought she was trying to get a pair of boots for me dad. So, they came and they measured my feet and found out that I did take a size nine shoe. She got twenty extra coupons because I wore a man's size boots. She sold them and from that day we had extra bacon and a bit of meat, all because I'd got big feet.

Bob Houghton, born 1936

Woollen Jerseys

My grandmother used to come down and take us to off down to Foster Brothers and fix us up with a shirt and a jersey. The jersey had a woollen tie knitted the same as the actual jersey and they would last you three years. I am sure it was barbed wire it was made of.

Dan Jones, born 1929

Work

In 1948, my father left my mother, I was twelve so I became the breadwinner. She was still doing other people's washing, she was still getting up at six o'clock in the morning and going down Rocky Lane and scrubbing floors and scrubbing steps and getting back in time to get us up to school.

Bob Houghton, born 1936

Brought Up by the Nurse

I had a nurse when I was a little lad of two. I was born in the First World War. My two brothers had been playing up, they'd be seven, I'd be two. My mother was crying her eyes out she said 'I don't know what to do with him' and this old

Stan Webb aged three in 1919. Stan's father owned three shops in Court Oak Road, Harborne.

lady said 'Wrap him up and I'll look after him'. And she happened to be the retired nurse of the Duke of Cambridge's children and she brought me up from when I was two to when I was about ten. I slept there, I lived there and my father used to give her meat from the butchers and grocery from the grocers to look after me. In fact I thought more of her than I did of my own mother.

Stanley Webb, born 1916

Divided Family

When I was eight my mum and dad told me we were coming to live in Birmingham. My father had come to get work in Hamstead Colliery at Great Barr

63

and he'd managed to get a pit house in Hamstead Village. Mum and I were coming to Birmingham to be with dad. Two nights before we left she said 'Tomorrow I'm taking you to meet a family where we got you from'. I said 'What do you mean?' She said 'The lady who gave birth to you and the man who is your real dad couldn't afford to keep you because they were very poor. Besides you, they'd got eight other children. One of them is a little girl called Jennifer and she is your twin sister. I want to take you to say goodbye to them before we go to Birmingham'. I did meet them and it was amazing to stand looking at her because it was like looking in a mirror. They all made a great fuss of me and hoped that my mum, the only mum that I ever knew, had come to bring me back. But I said 'I don't want to come back, I don't belong here'. The lady was holding my hands and crying and I was saying 'I don't want you to do that, you're making me feel like I am doing something wrong and I want to go with my mum'. So we came up to Birmingham.

Peggy Gilbert, born 1928

Grandparents

When I was a child in the '30s, a few weeks after your mother had given birth to you, your grandparents would look after you. It was the done thing that you grew up with your grandparents because your mother and father went to work. My mother and father worked six days a week.

George Turner, born 1932

Moonlight Flit

One night there was a man pushing a hand cart with all this furniture piled up and about five or six kids round it. I said to my father 'Where's he going with that lot at this time of night Dad?'

Miners' houses at Hamstead Colliery, Great Barr, c. 1910. Peggy Gilbert's family moved to the village in 1936 when her father got a job in the pit.

MINE FIRE HAMSTEAD COLLIERY, GREAT BARR, BIRMINGHAM MARCH 4TH 1908.

COLLIERY

J.WELSBY.

BARNSLEY DETACHMENT
TANKERSLEY BRIGADE
RESCUE PARTY.

CONSTRUCTING AIR PASSAGE.

MEN ENTOMBED

SAMUEL MITCHELL

RICHARD ASHTON ARTHUR P. CURTIS WALTER SUMMERFIELD

PUBLISHED BY W. GOTHARD, 6, ELDON STREET, BARNSLEY. COPYRIGHT

Postcard commemorating the men who died in the fire at Hamstead Colliery, Birmingham, 1908.

He said 'Son, he's doing a moonlight flit'. The man was moving house because he owed a load of rent on a house and he was only moving round the corner to another house.

Alfred Palmerfield, born 1927

The Chemist

In the '30s, there was no national health system. If you went to the doctors, you'd have to pay for it. My family, like a lot of other families, couldn't afford the doctors so most of the medical work was done at the local chemist. If there was something wrong with you, mother used to take you down to the chemist and he would have a look at you, and prescribe some medicine. You just couldn't afford to go to the doctors except in an emergency. During the war, we used to have a garden at school and we were digging up the ground and I put a fork through my foot. Me mother couldn't afford to take me to the doctors, so I went to the chemist and because he knew my mother, she didn't have to pay.

George Turner, born 1932

Paying the Doctor

A lot of people died of consumption because of bad diets and bad living conditions. Women died young because they were having too many children. There wasn't any medical care. There was a doctor, and if he come you paid him a shilling and if it was a death you give him 2s 6d. It wasn't until after the war until it really started to get good.

Northumberland Street after the War and before the redevelopment of Duddeston and Nechells.

There was no health service. So many people were dying because they didn't have the money to have the doctor in or go to the chemist. If you went to the doctor, or the doctor come to you, you had to pay. If you went to the chemist to buy stuff, you had to pay. Otherwise, if you didn't make it, you didn't make it and you died.

Peggy Gilbert, born 1928

Medical Advice

To be able to go to the doctor's, it would cost 2s 6d, and people couldn't afford it so they always used to come to my mother, who ran the pawn shop, for advice. She even used to make up cough syrups for them. She knew when people had measles or chicken pox or common ailments.

Renee Kingston, born 1918

Paying with Rations

The National Health Service made a lot of difference. During the war years, I remember the patient had to pay the hospital £2 for each delivery, and we midwives had to collect this money. When my colleague and I used to go out to collect our £2 from the mothers we had delivered, we often had rations given to us instead. Quite a lot of these women with families of ten or eleven, or even five or six would actually have more coupons than they had money to buy food. We could probably get half a pound of bacon, or a pound of butter or a packet of tea and we did not say 'No thank you'.

Ellen O'Brien, born 1911

CHAPTER 4

Food

The old Market Hall in the Bull
Ring, 1950. The Market Hall
suffered bomb damage during the
Blitz. After the Second World War,
it was left with no roof but was used
until it was demolished to make way
for the new shopping centre.

Marjorie Sanders and her parents, Rookery Road, Handsworth, 1937. The family did all their food shopping on Soho Road.

Shopping in Handsworth

In the late 1920s, when I was seven or eight, I used to go shopping with my mother on a Friday night. That was a ritual. Apart from doing some shopping, you always went to meet people. It was a social event to go down Handsworth main road. Mother would meet people that she knew socially and we'd stand there with perhaps three or four people talking together. There were few cars, you could just walk across. There was the Handsworth market where you could go – in the winter there would be great gas flares for illumination – these flickering, noisy great big flames that would enable you to see the money in your hand. There'd be fish stalls, vegetable stalls and remnants, and a big linen shop that sold towels and sheets.

Marjorie Sanders, born 1915

Queuing for Beer

We had a outdoor licensed premises not far from us and they used to queue up right past our window for this pub. There was one old lady and we'd see her go up and then a bit later on we'd see her go down with her jug of beer. Then she'd join the end of the queue and she'd stand in the queue and drink her beer and go and get another one.

Gwendoline Webb, born 1908

Kardomah Café

When you went down New Street, there were some lovely shops. I liked the Bull Ring when it was the old fashioned Bull Ring with the barrow boys. I used to go down there every time

I went to town. You'd get some lovely fruit and vegetables quite cheap especially if it was nearly half past four when they were clearing away. There was the Kardomah Café and I used to love to pass that because of the smell of the coffee being ground – you'd see the coffee grinder in the window grinding the coffee. It used to encourage you to go in and buy a cup of coffee.

Sadie Bryant, born 1907

Jam

I left school at fourteen in 1924 and I started work at a jam factory in Tiverton Road. I was there a week. My job was to wash all the jam jars. In those days, there weren't the 1lb jars of jam that we see on the shelves these days. They were big glass jars full of jam or marmalade and people used to take cups to the corner shop to buy 3d worth of jam.

Ruby Rhydderch, born 1910

Shop Work

We used to weigh the sugar up. When we got home from school we had a two hundredweight bag of sugar and we put it into blue bags. We used to have the butter in big slabs and if anybody wanted half a pound of butter you cut it. You cut the cheese on a wire. I could do all that when I was

The interior of the Kardomah Café, Birmingham, 1968.

Wai Lan Liu grows Chinese vegetables in the garden of her home in Belchers Lane, Alum Rock, 1980. As there were few specialist food shops in Birmingham, many newcomers to the city had difficulty in getting hold of their traditional foods.

Fish Market

Jewish women became very adept at producing excellent food with very little. There were one or two Jewish suppliers. We were such a large family and we had lots of visitors as well, sometimes there were as many as twelve or fifteen people to sit down for a meal. Every week, on Thursday afternoon, my mother would take me into town to the old Market Hall. I was about seven or eight. She would come back laden with fish. I remember outside the Market Hall, a man sat there with a wooden cask of salt herrings. We would come home by tram and bus, and she would stay up until three or four o'clock in the morning cooking fish, ready for the Sabbath and the weekend.

Paul Winter, born 1916

ten. We had bacon cut on the machine not in packets. People used to come and say 'Have you got a 6d packet?' Well, a 6d packet was all the odds and ends that you'd dropped in the sawdust and you rolled them up and put them on the counter.

Stanley Webb, born 1916

Rations

Food was rationed then – 2oz of bacon, one egg. We had a chicken that we kept in the house that laid eggs, but we couldn't tell anybody because they'd come and pinch the eggs.

Bob Houghton, born 1936

Food Shopping

We go to the Chinese supermarket to buy our cooking ingredients but now we want to venture out to other restaurants, not just go only to Chinese restaurants. Sometimes we try Indian restaurants, to have a Balti, or maybe Italian. The Chinese Quarter is not a place to live. It is full of restaurants. You go there to spend your money, to have your entertainment. We go to the Chinese supermarket a lot to do our shopping but also we visit the Bull Ring every week.

Wai Lan Liu, born 1953

Fish and Chips

My parents are both Greek Cypriot and they owned a fish and chip shop in Alum Rock. The fish and chip shop had unsociable hours. The language they had to know was very limited – simple phrases like 'Hello', 'Yes, please', 'Salt and vinegar?' It was family-orientated, they could be cooking chips with the kids growing up around them and they could earn money which reflected their hard work and unsociable hours. A lot of Greeks own fish and chip shops. When the price of potatoes is high, they sit together and say 'What are we going to do?' They share the stress and worry of the price of fish being high. You'll go to church and you'll hear them sitting in the back row, saying 'The fish was expensive this week'. When we have a party, we always say 'There's no talk about the price of fish or potatoes at this party!'

Gabriel Gabriel, born 1963

Corned Beef

Immediately opposite our shop was a hucksters shop which sold everything, a bit of corn beef, bread and milk. I remember our mother sending us across the road to buy 2d worth of corned beef and I remember going across and my tummy just turned over because it was full of maggots.

Renee Kingston, born 1918

Bacon

The sides of bacon and the hams were hung on hooks up the stairs

Ten Acres and Stirchley Co-op shop, Woodlands Park Road, Kings Norton, 1928.

and there they stayed until you wanted a slice off the bacon. None of us seemed to get ill and none of us died. You never had refrigerators to keep anything in, so how did we survive?

Rita Hancox, born 1937

Helping in the Shop

As a child, I remember the shop being very busy. We weren't allowed in the shop area until we were older. We were allowed to stack the shelves but that was about it. We weren't allowed to talk to the customers. My dad used to run the shop and my granddad used to sit with him.

We didn't have much interaction with the customers. Dad always used to say "Keep it professional. If you start becoming personal with them, they'll want credit from you'. As we got older, we were encouraged to stay in the shop. The shop changed face many times. Initially it was a grocery shop, then a newsagent, then wines and spirits. My dad kept adding on to the shop to make it bigger and better. None of us wanted to do shop work because it was a seven-day job.

Avtar Tulwar, born 1969

The Tulwar family, in 1971. At that time, the whole family lived together in Court Road, Balsall Heath and owned a local shop. Avtar is the little girl on the left.

Stan Webb aged fourteen in 1930. At sixteen, Stan's father put him in charge of the family's butchers shop.

Meat Market

In about 1928, we used to go every morning to the market at half past five. We used to walk round the market and watch all the butchers working. Then dad would drop us off in Harborne in time for the opening of school. The meat market was in Bradford Street. You can imagine hundreds of sides of beef hanging up and slaughterhouses where they used to kill all the livestock. Major butchers used to carry a big handful of wood skewers and if they fancied a side of beef or a lamb, they'd put the skewer into it and nobody would bother to buy that, it was spoken for by the butcher whose skewer was in it. Having three shops, my mother had to look after the shops while he was down the market buying the meat so the three kids had to go down. We used to get our breakfast in the market. We used to have dripping buns for 1s 2d. There was a big tea urn, eggs, bacon and sausages.

Stanley Webb, born 1916

5d of Liver

We used to hang the meat until it was dark. It was tender then. We had no fridges, we had ice boxes. We had a big wooden box and we used to put chopped up ice and sawdust in it and

73

keep the meat in there. On Saturday night, we had the window open and we put all the meat out on the window and I'd be there shouting 'Lovely shoulder of lamb, 10d'. The people in the big houses, they used to send the chauffeur in for 5d of liver 'for the dog' but it was for the husband's tea.

Stanley Webb, born 1916

Allotment

My father always had an allotment so I never used to know what it was like to go to a greengrocer's shop except for things like oranges, apples and bananas. There was always home-grown cauliflowers, cabbage, beans, onions and potatoes. I was well fed with those. My mother used to pickle eggs in a big jar so we'd always got eggs from the fowl that we kept. We did that during the war because things were very, very short. These eggs were kept in a solution in a big crock jar kept in the pantry. A good many people in suburbia kept fowl in the garden especially during the war. My husband kept rabbits and we used to eat those. I used to love the rabbits so that I couldn't eat them without a tear dropping down. Sometimes I just couldn't eat them.

Marjorie Sanders, born 1915

Sunday Lunch

When I was young in the late '60s, early '70s, Sunday lunch was always meat and two vegetables, gravy and then a pudding. I was never very keen on vegetables and my dad always insisted that I ate them. He used to

74

make me stay at the table until I'd eaten them, and they could have been cold. With my own children, I am not going to make them eat. I always get them to try something but I don't insist.

Maria Finch, born 1963

Family Meals

When we go to my grandparents' house, we always eat curries because that's what my nan cooks. We eat traditionally western food. Every Sunday, we have roast dinner but, once a fortnight, my mum does cook a curry or an Asian meal which we all enjoy because my father eats them as well.

Lara Coles, born 1983

Irish Food

Even though I was born in this country, I was brought up on good Irish food. We usually had potatoes and we ate the skins of the potatoes because they were the best part of the potato. We had soda bread, the colcannon, the gravy, the meat and two veg. Mum always made sure that we sat down round the table in the evenings. The TV went off and we talked about the day. Dad had a fry up on his weekend off with white pudding, black pudding and soda bread, and any other meat he could fit on the plate.

Martha McCarron, born 1972

A stand at the Birmingham Show in Handsworth Park shows produce grown on the city's allotments.

Eating Together

Sunday, we try to sit down together. Four, five times a week we'll sit down together and eat. The children don't want to stay at the table and talk, they want to go and watch television or they want to go and play in their bedroom. My oldest Sarah does her homework or she'll be on the phone to her friends. In my own childhood, we always sat down to eat on a Sunday.

Maria Finch, born 1963

Eating in the Nineties

Children now tend to be more fussy because everything is so much quicker. Sitting down and eating a Macdonald's, seems so much more appealing than sitting down and eating roast potatoes or meat and two veg. I think society in general has made children more finicky because it is easier to go and buy a quick snack that's not very healthy than prepare something for yourself. They just want to eat and run. My children don't eat school dinners, they take a packed lunch because I know that they wouldn't eat what they put in front of them.

Maria Finch, born 1963

Rice and Peas

We were used to yam, bananas, sweet potatoes and rice. When we came here we found that English people did not use rice the way we did. They used it to make rice pudding but we made rice and peas. Rice was our staple diet with other things added such as yam and sweet potatoes. We had meat and fish. We ate a lot of fish at home but the fish was different here because our fish was tropical fish. Some of our people

Princes Corner, Harborne, in the 1930s.

didn't like it and they would say 'We don't like this food'. I made the change over quite easily and I got to like English cooking.

Dan Lawrence, born 1922

A Jewish Table

My mother was a very religious woman, a pious woman. On the Sabbath, the table was properly laid with the candles and she blessed the candles as the Sabbath came in. She kept a Jewish table. The food was all Kosher with everything kept separate – milk and meat. There were always two lots of dishes which meant an enormous extra amount of work. Then, once a year, there was Passover. Everything that has been used for everyday purposes has to be disposed of, every crumb has to be cleared. A new set of dishes has to come out. Everything is new and is marked by the authorities as suitable for the Passover. It was a lovely time but a great deal of work.

Paul Winter, born 1916

Confirmation Pledge

I didn't start drinking until I was eighteen because I took my pledge. When I was confirmed, I made a promise that I wouldn't drink until after I was eighteen. My English friends hadn't heard of the pledge. They used to be out drinking away but I didn't feel any pressure.

Martha McCarron, born 1972

A shop on Harborne High Street, 1922.

German Food

Even today, I still like German food to the extent that when we go over to Calais, I've got an unholy tendency to smuggle food back in with me, especially all these strong cheeses and the salamis and sauerkraut. When I go to Germany to see my cousin, the one thing I look forward to more than anything else is the food which you can't get over here. The trouble is it's so expensive, so when I do go abroad, I smuggle the stuff back with me and stock up.

Jack Driels, born 1923

West Indian Food

We had some West Indian food at home but not as much as I would have liked. We tended to eat more West

Indian food when we were at other people's houses rather than our own house. As a result, I haven't really learned how to cook anything apart from the basic dishes. My son is being brought up with a wide knowledge of both. He loves Jamaican food and West Indian food. His nan cooks a lot more of it for him than she did for me which is good because he really enjoys it.

Malika Ahmed, born 1967

Chinese Food

Despite the fact that we live here for so long, we still like Chinese food. The children will not like fish and chips. Sometimes I don't want to cook. I suggest to them 'How about we just buy some fish and chips or go to Macdonald's'. They say 'No way'. They still love Chinese cooking. We eat rice every day and we like fresh vegetables. We like seafood. On the whole, our cooking is Chinese. We do not cook much English food. I will enjoy an English meal but not my children, nor my husband. He will say 'Oh, I like my Chinese food'.

Wai Lan Liu, born 1953

School Dinners

I've been a dinner lady at Elm's Farm Junior and Infant school for thirty years. I started in 1968. Lunchtime was an important part of the school day. Children were expected to learn manners, to be able to sit at the table and to be able to use a knife and fork. It was all laid out properly. They weren't rushed. They had to say grace beforehand 'For what we are about to receive, may the Lord make us truly thankful'. All the children said 'Amen'

Wai Lan Liu dines with her family in a Birmingham Balti restaurant, 1998.

and couldn't sit down quick enough. Dinners were set meals – meat and two veg, fish, steak and kidney pudding. Everything was made and cooked by the cook herself. She decided on the menus. She was in total control. It began to change in the late '80s. The school lunch hours were cut, so instead of being a social occasion, it was a case of 'the children have got to have a meal but we need the time for other things'. The meals come pre-packed. The cooks missed the responsibility of preparing the meals, deciding what the children liked and didn't like.

Wendy Fenn, born 1942

Curry and Chapatis

As an Asian child you grow up with curries and chapatis which are very good for you. My sister cooked after my mother died in 1976. She had to learn very quickly. She was taught by a relative of ours and she got better and better. My wife Janjeet is a very good cook. I've got taste for other foods as well. I like Italian food and especially West Indian food. With West Indian food it is very similar to Asian cooking because it is very spicy and I love spicy food. I do quite like wines. The children quite like eating Asian food but we give them a balanced diet. We probably have curry two or three times a week. Other than that, we eat bland English food, mainly convenience food.

Gurdip Gill, born 1969

Taste of Germany

I haven't actually lived in Germany for such a long time, but it has an emotional hold on you. I buy German bread, German sausage and gherkins. The food takes you back there without actually going there. You've got the taste of the country. Once you taste that food, it triggers something off in your mind. My grandmother would send us parcels of food in the early '50s because Britain was still on rationing and yet there was no rationing in Germany. We always used to look forward to the parcels because they smelled different somehow. She'd send us vanilla sugar, black bread and sausages.

Georg Hands, born 1947

School Dinners

When I was at infant school when I was five or six in about 1968, I can remember I had my meal at school. The meals were cooked on the school site and we had ladies that looked after us during the lunch hour, the dinner supervisors. We never called them by their first name. You had a tray, you had a plate and you had a bowl for your pudding then you had to collect your knife and fork at the end of the queue. There was this big dinner supervisor and I was so frightened of her. She must have taken a shine to me because I was a weedy little child, ever so thin, and she used to stand behind me and place her hands on my shoulders, and say to the lady dishing out the cabbage and the carrots 'Put this one extra. She needs fattening up'. She'd insist that I

A formal approach to school dinners, *c.* 1940s. (Courtesy of Birmingham Post and Mail)

eat it and I used to be so upset, every dinner time. In the end, I had to tell my mum why I didn't want to go to school. So she had to ring the school and tell them not to make me eat my cabbage and carrots.

Maria Finch, born 1963

Dinner Lady

When we were children, we were told we had to eat everything but I never did that as a dinner lady. That was something I vowed I would never do. I would never sit a child down and say 'You've got to eat that. You've got to clear your plate'. I'd rather say 'Well go on, have a try, it's a new thing. If you don't like it, you haven't got to eat it'. Otherwise you've lost them. They'll leave the whole meal and they can end up in tears. To me, the dinner hour is an important part of their life. It's a social part for them.

Wendy Fenn, born 1942

CHAPTER 5
Pioneers

Larry Finglass, aged ten in 1956, two years before his family moved to Birmingham from Ireland.

Jack Driels with his primary school class in Ladenburg, Germany, aged five in 1928 (seated, first left). Jack came to England alone in 1938, aged fifteen, to escape Nazi persecution of Jewish people. Two of his classmates (standing, second right and seated, second left) escaped in 1939 and walked to Israel.

Move from Ireland

When I left school at fourteen, I had a good job as a trainee carpenter and all of a sudden my dad decided to come to England in 1958. He'd got a job in one of the car industries and in 1960, he decided that all the family would move. I was sixteen at the time and really looking forward to it, coming from the country into a big city but yet missing Ireland so much, it was unbelievable. I used to count the seconds sometimes till I went back home. It took me quite a few years to settle down.

Larry Finglass, born 1946

Jewish Refugee

I first came to England in 1938. I was born in Ladenburg which is a small village in Baden in Germany. The Nazis came during the night, took all male Jewish people including my father and my uncle. They were taken to the market square where there was an open lorry and sent to Dachau concentration camp. And whilst they were in the market square, the population who we always thought of as friends, pelted them with stones and mud. Because I was under age, I wasn't taken, everybody else was. I was put on a train towards the end of 1938, on a Children's Transport, to England. I came to a place called Birmingham, which I hadn't

82

heard of before, and I was just fifteen then. I was a little bit bewildered. When I left Germany, I used to fight the kids in the street because I was a Jew and when I came to Birmingham and started in the factory, I was fighting in the factory because I was a German. So whatever happened, I didn't win.

Jack Driels, born 1923

Parents from Pakistan

My parents came over in the '60s because the British government ran a recruitment campaign to get people to work in the foundries.

Avtar Tulwar, born 1969

Windrush

I was born in Jamaica in the year 1922 so I am now seventy-six. I would call myself a pioneer because I came over with the first exodus of Caribbean people to this country in '48. I came over on the *Windrush*, a troop ship. I wanted to see the country that influenced my education very greatly and my values in life. Most of us were young men who just came over on a wave of excitement to try life out in a new country. There were a few older men who had worked in England during the war. They went back home to Jamaica and they couldn't settle down there so they came back on the boat with us.

Dan Lawrence, born 1922

Dan Lawrence arrived in England from Jamaica on the *Empire Windrush* in 1948.

Setting up a Business

My father was a Jewish immigrant from Poland. He came here in the early 1900s. He married and had three children and in giving birth to the third child, his wife died. My mother was about twenty-four and he took her in as a housekeeper to look after the children and a year later he married her and on the second of December 1916, I appeared. He worked very hard. Jewish people were barred from many, many trades which is why so many of them were in finance or the textile trade. He opened up a little shop in Balsall Heath and he progressed to a four-storey factory opposite the old meat market. On the ground floor was the shop and stores, and on the next two floors were work rooms where there were about thirty or forty people, and on the top floor there was a flat where we lived.

Paul Winter, born 1916

Parents from Ireland

My mother and father are Irish. My mother came from Mayo and my father came from Donegal. They came over to England in the '60s looking for work. They met over here and got married in 1970 and I arrived in 1972.

Martha McCarron, born 1972

Dan Lawrence as pictured on his British Jamaican passport issued in 1948.

Furthering a Career

We had come from a country where we couldn't go back really. I couldn't go back, after leaving my job and my country and persuading my family that I was coming here to further my career, I wouldn't go back and face them. I wanted to go back in the first few months. I didn't like it here because I didn't get suitable jobs. I was homesick really. It made me think 'Why did I come?' because I had a wonderful life back home. I didn't have high expectations when I came here. My aim was to earn money and support my family and also get some further education. It was more of an economic necessity to come to England.

Mohammed Ayyub, born 1939

Portrait from the Dyche Collection.

Cold Summers

When we came to England, we landed at Tilbury Docks in London and it was a very cold day. It was in June but unfortunately it was not a summer's day. It was rather cold and chilly, and my first impression was 'How do people manage to live in this country at this time of year, it being so cold?'

Dan Lawrence, born 1922

Sharing a Room

Where I used to live in Farm Road there were eleven lodgers living in one house. And we were three friends living in one big room, cooking in the same room as well. Housing was a problem for the Asians, they couldn't buy their own homes. They used to be lodgers and they couldn't afford to pay a lot of rent.

Mohammed Ayyub, born 1939

British Food

I spoke broken English when I started in the factory. My uncle put me in the YMCA in Bristol Street. I was there on my own, getting on for fifteen. I did not eat anything for two weeks, I wasn't used to British food at all. I had a bit of money and luckily enough opposite the YMCA there was a Wimbush's and they were selling cream cakes and I existed

For many migrants, a photograph was an important way of showing friends and relatives back home that they were finding success in England. (From the Dyche Collection)

The Dyche photographic studio in Balsall Heath was used by many people who settled in Birmingham. The studio provided props for some of its customers – including whisky bottles.

Jack Driels' classmates at the Real-Gymasium, Ladenburg (preparatory school for Heidelburg University), 1937. Jack and the other Jewish pupils in his class were not allowed to appear in the photograph.

for two weeks on cream cakes.

Jack Driels, born 1923

Learning to Cook

We had to cook ourselves. I was not prepared for it, I had never cooked at home. In my country, girls, sisters and mothers cook and we weren't prepared for it. But we had to start learning it. We used to make chapatis and we used to make curry. It was very smelly for the other lodgers who used to live in the same flats – West Indian and English guys. They used to hate our curry smell. We didn't like the smell of their West Indian fish.

Mohammed Ayyub, born 1939

Wendy Fenn goes for a paddle, with her dress tucked into her knickers, aged six in Sidbury, Devon, 1948.

Hard Work

My father came here just after the Second World War from the Punjab in India and my mother followed on five years after that. My father tells us stories of when he first came to England. He can look back and laugh about some of the things that happened, about sharing a house with twenty people. There is a great affinity with the Irish. The Irish would tell them 'Since the immigrants came, you've taken the pressure off us'. He didn't know any English when he first came here. He would try and save money to bring my mother over. He started work in a foundry. Because he was trying to save hard and send money home to his family, he used to work a twelve hour day in a foundry and then go door-to-door selling. That's how he saved money. My mother came over, then my father started a family and I am the youngest of six children.

Gurdip Gill, born 1969

Arrival from Devon

When I first came to Birmingham at the age of eleven in 1953, I came from a little quiet village which was Sidbury just outside Sidmouth and to come to Birmingham, it was terrifying. It was traffic, it was lots of people, not knowing anybody, a strange school. I had a broad Devonshire accent, so making myself understood didn't help me.

Wendy Fenn, born 1942

Coming from Jamaica

I was born in Jamaica in 1955 and I came to England in 1962. My mother left me at the age of three and went to England. I was left with friends of the family. They reckoned they'd come to England to make a better life for themselves, much better than the life they were living in Jamaica. When I first came to England, I found it horrendous. The houses were so tiny and looked like factories, with smoking chimneys. I just wasn't used to all that. When I came to England, I was around the age of seven. It was December, close to Christmas, and my first impressions were absolutely awful. I'd left Jamaica in a little summer outfit, with a nice little hat. It was horrid because it was so cold. I had no coat. Our parents didn't meet us at the airport because they'd arranged for us to be picked up and brought down to Birmingham. By the time we got to Birmingham it was very dark at night and I was really tired. I was thinking 'Where is my house?' Then one of the doors opened and mum and dad stood there, I nearly died. Although they were joyous to see me, I thought 'This is awful, I want to go home'. I remembered mum very vaguely, I was very young when she left me so I just vaguely remembered her, and my dad was like a complete stranger.

Shirley, born 1955

Alum Rock

When I first arrived in Birmingham in 1979, we lived in Alum Rock. It looked to me like a little town.

Wendy Fenn's parents moved from Sidbury in Devon to Birmingham when she was eleven. Wendy (on the left) is pictured with two friends in the garden of her home in Church Road, Sheldon, not long after the family moved there.

Everywhere there were houses, no high rises. There were big fields down in Yardley Green. Where we lived, there is a little shopping area in Alum Rock called Belcher's Lane. There were a lot of Asians there and a lot of Asian shops. I liked it because I am Asian so I felt quite at home because in Hong Kong, we also have Indian Asian people there. At that time, I did not venture out a lot. My area was quite small – just my workplace and the market. It was a nice city. I quite liked it, not too rural. Because I come from Hong Kong, I like the city.

Wai Lan Liu, born 1953

Homesickness

When I first came to Birmingham, I was quite lonely. You've got to make friends. There was a terrible feeling of homesickness and you wonder why you left home in the first instance. If you can't live where you are, you'd never survive.

Bryan Kelly, born 1931

Sparkhill

When my parents first came over, they lived in Sparkhill. There was quite a large Irish community there. The Irish found it quite difficult to find accommodation. There was more Irish than English living in Sparkhill when I was growing up in the '70s. They did support each other. They were very close knit. They needed each other. A lot of the women went into nursing and cleaning and the men went into the building industry.

Martha McCarron, born 1972

Invited to Tea

My friend and I were out one day walking across the park and we met a very nice Englishman. He was nice but he was curious too because he said he had never met coloured people before and he invited us to visit his home which was in Smethwick. We felt excited about visiting an English home for the first time.

Dan Lawrence, born 1922

Getting on with Brummies

All the lads I work with are all Brummies, one or two Irish and

Wai Lan Liu outside her house in Belchers Lane, Alum Rock in 1980.

Pakistanis and Jamaicans. Very easy going, they are tremendous people. I really like being among the Brummie people now, I really like the Brummie accent.

Larry Finglass, born 1946

Neighbours

I was born in South Wales but I've spent most of my life in Birmingham but I'm afraid I haven't lost my Welsh accent. The next door people didn't speak to me for a year which I found very funny because I knew everyone in Wales – every time I went out, I knew people. So one day, I said 'Why haven't you spoken to me, I've been here a year and you've never spoken to me and I find that very difficult'. She said 'Well, the people who lived there before you, we didn't like them'. After that, they were lovely neighbours.

Sadie Bryant, born 1907

Attitudes to Immigrants

I think I got on more with the immigrants in Birmingham than I did with the Birmingham people themselves. It was only later that I got on with the Birmingham people. I always thought they were anti people coming into their city. That's the feeling I always got.

Bryan Kelly, born 1931

Bryan Kelly in 1955, not long after arriving in Birmingham.

Curiosity

We found that people were very curious about black people and some of them actually were running away from us. They ran inside the house, they closed the door and they went to the window, having a good look at us but they wouldn't come out to see us at all. They wouldn't come out to meet us. It was a very strange experience to see people actually running from us.

Dan Lawrence, born 1922

Racism

Our generation had never seen a black person, only at the pictures or in books. When I was a little girl, if you did anything really naughty, I can remember my mum used to say 'If you don't behave yourself, the black man's going to get you'. So of course, when the Afro-Caribbeans came in the '50s, I was a bit apprehensive and a little bit frightened. I used to go dancing at the West End when the first black fellows used to be there and I was really frightened. It's just ridiculous, I was frightened in case one asked me to dance. I didn't know what to say, yes or no. That's how you were brought up. It was racism, it was ridiculous, stupid and prejudiced. My elder son, his partner is Sikh so I've got a granddaughter of mixed race, she's nearly three and she's absolutely beautiful.

Norma Morgan, born 1937

Choosing a Church

When we first came to Birmingham, we felt if we want to make it home, we need to mix with the local people. So we deliberately go to a local English church, not to the Chinese church. If you want to make it home, you need to break away, to mix with the local people. You cannot enclose yourself within your own community. The church we go to is an inner city church in Small Heath, there are some white but the majority are West Indian. We feel comfortable there.

Wai Lan Liu, born 1953

Asian Films

We were starved for music. There was no way to get our music from India and Pakistan. There were no cinemas showing Asian films at that time. People were thrilled to get any kind of records and play them. We used to travel all the way to Bradford to buy records. In 1966, we bought a television set but there was no Asian programmes. There were cinemas which showed Asian films in the early '60s, as matinee shows in the English cinemas. Matinee shows were held on Sundays. That was the best entertainment Asians could hope for at the time. Our people were

A nurse, Dyche Collection.

lonely and homesick without their families. They used to gather there, discuss their problems, and read their letters from back home. They used to dress nicely. It was a social get-together for them. They would come long before the film started and have a get-together.

Mohammed Ayyub, born 1939

Jobs in Jamaica

The car industry wouldn't employ black people in the early '50s. I couldn't get a job there, I was turned down. Many of the workers did not have my level of education but they were offered better jobs. Jobs were very plentiful at that time. That was so much different from how things were at home. At home if you had a job, you had to keep it. If you lost it, it would take you months to get another one.

Dan Lawrence, born 1922

Getting a Job

When I was demobbed in 1952, I found it was hard to find work in Liverpool. So in 1955 at the age of twenty-four, I jumped on the train and headed for Birmingham. I remember getting off the train at New Street and getting a local paper. I was amazed when I saw how many vacancies there were. I found digs and work on the same day. I started work the following morning at the Rotunda building site which was just starting. It was a hole in the ground. Within the first week, I had three jobs. I was amazed how much work there was

Bryan Kelly found work helping to build the Rotunda when he first came to Birmingham in 1955.

in Birmingham. It surprised me how many immigrants there were in the Midlands as compared to Liverpool. Then it dawned on me that the reason these people were here was because of the work.

Bryan Kelly, born 1931

West Midlands Transport

I was born in 1939 in Punjab which is now Pakistan and I travelled on 7 December 1961. I was excited to come here, I didn't know what type of place it was going to be. I tried to find a job here but I couldn't get any job at all. I ultimately applied in the West Midlands transport for a conductor's job. My degree from Punjab wasn't recognised so it was useless. Being a graduate, I didn't want to do that job but I was forced. Most of the people turned us away from the gate, they said 'No jobs'. It was a surprise because we had heard stories that English were very decent. We were called Pakis on the buses when I was working there. Most of the passengers were decent but there were some who were racist. Some used to abuse us.

Mohammed Ayyub, born 1939

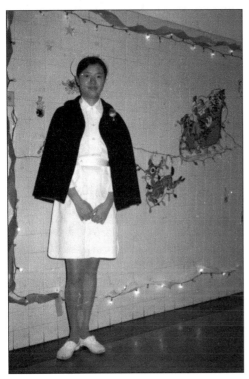

Although the training for nurses in Hong Kong was based on the British system, Wai Lan Liu's nursing qualifications were not recognised in England. Here, she is a trainee general nurse in Hong Kong's Kwong Wah Hospital aged twenty-one in 1975.

Prejudice at Work

There was a lot of prejudice in employment. Employers were willing to give you a job, if it was a very low paid job and didn't have any promotion prospect. They were quite willing to give you that job. You would go for other jobs and they would say 'I am sorry, no vacancies' but the vacancies were on the board out there.

Dan Lawrence, born 1922

First Day

It was arranged that the factory manager was going to pick me up in the mornings, take me to work, and bring me home. On the very first day of me going to work, which was the day after I arrived in Birmingham, I did not know what a factory was, I did not know what time they start or finish or how many hours they worked. I was on a pavement outside the YMCA, it must have been January '39, at six o'clock in the morning, because I didn't know what time they started. The factory manager arrived at ten o'clock.

Jack Driels, born 1923

Qualifications

When I first started work, because all my education and qualifications were in Hong Kong they were not recognised in this country, I looked for work as a non-qualified person. My first job was as a cleaner in an adult training centre. When I first came to the UK in the 1970s and I realised all my education and qualifications were not recognised, I felt very bitter about it. I have to say I cried a lot for the first three to four years. I thought 'Over ten years study and training completely down the drain. All my hard work and now I come to this country and I have to re-train'. I felt it was unfair because in Hong Kong the nursing system followed exactly the UK system. In Hong Kong we sat the same exams. I felt it was discrimination. It took me quite a few years to get over this hurt and pain.

Wai Lan Liu, born 1953

Birmingham Accent

The Birmingham accent, I couldn't understand it whatsoever. My first job was in New Street Station in the telegraph office and of course most of them were all Brummie lads and I couldn't understand a word they were saying. Except there was one, Andy Turner, who was married to an Irish girl and he was the only one I could understand. He used to have to pass the messages on.

Larry Finglass, born 1946

Irish Loyalties

I'm very proud to be Irish. My lads have a problem when Ireland play England because I'm sitting in one corner shouting for Ireland and they're keeping quiet. I'm still Irish when they are playing England but when England are playing anybody else, I want England to win. I haven't got divided loyalties because I want Ireland to win, end of story.

Larry Finglass, born 1946

Pakistani Loyalties

I am British as much as I am living here but I have my roots back home which are very deep. When England and Pakistan are playing cricket, my feelings are always that Pakistan should win but when England is playing West Indies or Australia, I would love England to win. When Aston Villa is playing Manchester United, I would like Aston Villa to win.

Mohammed Ayyub, born 1939

Internationalist

I see myself as an internationalist. I wouldn't say that I am West Indian any more than I am British. I just take the best of what I see in any people.

Dan Lawrence, born 1922

Liverpool Loyalties

I've been in Birmingham now, must be over forty years. And like the salmon we always remember our home, so my home is still Liverpool. I'm still a Scouser. All the children are Brummies. Some of them support Aston Villa. I still support Liverpool.

Bryan Kelly, born 1931

Chinese Loyalties

I came to the UK in 1979 and my husband came three years before me, so we have lived in Birmingham all this time, coming up for twenty years now. For me, I will say, despite living in UK for so long, I still see myself as Chinese. We mix very well with local people. We have a local church, we feel we belong to the church. We feel we belong to the community here but we still feel we are Chinese. No matter how good your English or how well you integrate in to society, once you walk out the door, people will say you are Chinese. That is a fact. I feel quite comfortable about this.

Wai Lan Liu, born 1953

Having left Germany as a child in 1938 as a Jewish refugee, Jack Driels joined the Argyll and Sutherland Highlanders in 1942. He was given British citizenship on joining the Army.

Going Home

I got to know from the International Red Cross how my parents and my family perished. The very first time I went back I was still in the Army. It was 1945 and I wanted to see if any member of our community had returned. Not one of them had. Because it was a small village there was no damage at all and nothing had changed and that upset me because I would have loved to have seen it smashed to pieces.

Jack Driels, born 1923

Blow-in

I have a problem when I go back to Ireland because they perceive me as English when I go back – or as a blow-in. I love going back to Ireland for my holidays. I go twice a year but I probably wouldn't stop there now. I feel more Brummie in the sense that I am quite happy stopping here now. But for twenty-five, maybe thirty years, the only thing that kept me going was to go back to live in Ireland. But eventually you get to accept it. I enjoy it here now. My children have got Brummie accents so when we go back on holidays to Ireland we are treated as Brummies.

Larry Finglass, born 1946

Coming Home

I went to America and I spent some time there. When I came back to England, I felt like I was coming home. But if I go back to Jamaica now I really

Larry and Nuala Finglass on their wedding day at the Rosary Church, Saltley, March 1968.

don't feel that I am really going home because I've lived here so long. My grandchildren do not find any direct connection with the West Indies.

Dan Lawrence, born 1922

First Home

Birmingham is my home and I feel strange if I go out of Birmingham. Even if I go to Pakistan, I would like to come back here because this is my first home now.

Mohammed Ayyub, born 1939

Being a Scouser

When I go to Liverpool now, I'm not accepted as a Scouser any more. I remember going to Liverpool about ten years ago. I went into a local pub and I tried to chat up Scousers because I was going to see Liverpool play Birmingham at Anfield. The Brummies on the train knew I was a Scouser and I went off on my own to mix with my fellow breed but they didn't accept me because to them, I wasn't a Scouser, I didn't sound like a Scouser. On that day Birmingham beat Liverpool 4-1 and I was so humiliated that I wouldn't get the same train back because I couldn't put up with all the chatter from the Birmingham supporters.

Bryan Kelly, born 1931

Going Home: Cyprus

My parents' initial intentions were to come over in the '50s, work for

97

Bryan Kelly's extended family in Birmingham, 1998.

ten years and go back to Cyprus. There was a labour shortage in the '50s. A few Greek people came then they used to sign in the other Greeks. They said 'We're going to work ten years and then go back' but a lot of them haven't gone back. Some of them who have got to retirement have gone back and have come back hurt because it is not the same place and it's like they're lost. They couldn't settle there, it's not the same country.

Gabriel Gabriel, born 1963

Problems Settling

I don't think I'd ever contemplate going to live in Germany permanently. One of the reasons is that after my father died, my mother went to live in Germany. She hadn't lived in Germany since she was eighteen or nineteen which was over forty years ago and when she went back, she couldn't settle down because things had totally changed. The people had changed that she knew. She only lasted nine months, then she had to come back. Most of the people that she loved were over here in England.

Georg Hands, born 1947

Home

When the family get together, they talk of home. My mother says she is going home in the summer. Home is somewhere she hasn't lived permanently for thirty-five-odd years.

Dave Harte, born 1968

CHAPTER 6
Belonging

Avtar Tulwar (second from right), Heathmount Primary School, Balsall Heath, 1978.

Greek Culture

When we were out of the house, we were very English, but within the four walls of our own homes, we were Greek. We used to eat Greek food, our houses had bits of Greek culture on the walls – you might have a couple of icons of the Virgin Mary on the walls, or something we brought back from Cyprus. There was no racism that we felt around us but we kept our culture within our four walls.

Gabriel Gabriel, born 1963

Mixed Race

My mother's Asian and my father is white. My mother's parents are Hindu. They were both born in the Gujerat in India and they moved over here about forty-five years ago. I can't class myself as fully Asian or fully white and I never have. If someone asked me what race I am, I'd say I'm mixed race. We had a discussion once that I am half-caste but I find half-caste offensive. Now I understand the meaning of it, I find it offensive so I prefer to be called mixed race. I think it sounds nicer than half-caste as well.

Lara Coles, born 1983

Asian Culture

There are difficulties in raising our children in this culture because we have to teach them our Asian way of life as well as them learning the Western way of life in school and college. They meet their friends, they speak English. We try to teach them our own language, our own way of life so they are split between two cultures. But if you are not too strict with them they can learn both ways of life. It can be beneficial to them rather than being detrimental. Some families are very strict and they don't allow their children to mix with the Western way of life and that is where the clash starts and that is where the trouble starts.

Mohammed Ayyub, born 1939

Loss of Identity

It is very important for a person to know their roots and their identity. I have come across a lot of second generation born in UK, they have lost their sense of identity. The older generation find it very difficult to accept the second generation of British-born Chinese. They think that, despite their skin colour, inside they are white. And the second generation find it difficult to integrate into the older generation because they cannot speak the language. They also realise their white counterparts will see them as Chinese, no matter how British they are. In one sense, they have lost their identity. They cannot identify purely with the white, they cannot identify completely with the Chinese. I hope they realise they are Chinese by blood but by nationality, they are British. I think my children feel they are Brummies. Birmingham is their home.

Wai Lan Liu, born 1953

Attitudes

I was the eldest daughter-in-law and my in-laws had an image of the perfect bride. They had an image of me as very traditional but my attitude is very forward thinking. I remember being told that I think like a white person.

Avtar Tulwar, born 1969

Racism

In my school, it doesn't matter what race you are because I don't think there is any racism around. It's never been any problem that my father's white and I look Asian. Because there are so many mixed race families in my area, it doesn't mean that you get so many strange looks when you are walking down the street with your father.

Lara Coles, born 1983

Caribbean Culture

I wasn't brought up with as much Caribbean culture as I would have liked. I would have liked to have got even more of it than I did. It was just snippets and bits here and there. My mother decided to try and put that behind her when she came here. I think it was to help her assimilate into the general population and seem less of a fish out of water. The only time I actually ever heard my mother speak Jamaican patois round the house was when she was very, very angry and then she spoke it so fast. We'd say to her 'What do people in Jamaica dress like? What do they eat?' and she'd say 'The same as over here, don't be silly'. But we knew it was different because we'd seen books and pictures.

Malika Ahmed, born 1967

Assembly

I went to Five Ways Grammar School which was a popular school for Jewish boys. At morning service, the Jewish boys would stand outside in the corridor from the main assembly while the rest of the boys were singing hymns. There were perhaps forty or fifty Jewish boys standing there and then the doors would open and someone would say 'Let the Jews in'. It was the phrasing that was anti-Semitic. People would say 'That Jew, Paul' without any intention to be offensive but in a way it is offensive. They didn't say 'That Roman Catholic, Mike'.

Paul Winter, born 1916

College

At Cadbury College there was a mixture of people. I was the only Irish person there. I went round mainly with Asian girls and I made very good friends with one Asian girl who I am still very close to. We got on really well because even though she was from Pakistan, her values were very similar to mine. I felt more understood by her than I did with my English friends.

Martha McCarron, born 1972

Malika Ahmed, working as a jazz singer, 1998.

Feeling at Home

I haven't felt at home in England for a very, very long time perhaps since I started becoming more aware of things, maybe from an early age when our next door neighbours would say things like 'Where were you born? And I'd say 'Birmingham'. And they'd say 'No, where were you born in Jamaica?' 'I wasn't born in Jamaica, I was born in Birmingham'. They'd say 'But your parents are Jamaican aren't they, so you're not English, you're Jamaican aren't you?' It was a way of constantly re-enforcing the fact that you were here but you weren't really part of the society and the culture here. Now, I'm in my thirties and I still don't feel at home. I live here and I work here but if I had the choice, I'd live and work in the Caribbean where I do feel at home.

Malika Ahmed, born 1967

Wedding

My sister got married in 1980. We were all dancing in the garden and the neighbours from next door decided to throw stones into our garden to stop us from dancing. My brother ran out and said 'Why did you do that?' They said 'You're making too much noise. You should learn to control your people. You're behaving like animals'. I thought to myself 'We're dancing. It's a wedding'. Things got out of hand and my uncle ended up fighting with the neighbour.

Avtar Tulwar, born 1969

Party Interrupted

We lived on the fourth floor of this building and there was a side entrance that lead up to the flat. I would have been about seven, my brother was eighteen months younger and then there was the baby. One night, my uncle, who we loved madly, came to see us. He'd brought us presents. We were laughing and joking and screaming with pleasure and my mother heard a noise and looked out of the window. There was an enormous mass of people looking up. Then there was a knock on the door and up came a policeman to have a look round. Apparently someone passing by had heard all this screaming coming from these premises where they knew Jews lived. They had reported it to the police that children were being ill-treated and the police came. The policeman came upstairs and saw this jolly, happy family scene and he went down and said to the woman who made the complaint 'Do you have any children?' and she said 'Yes' and he said 'Go home and look after them as well as these children are being looked after'.

Paul Winter, born 1916

Grandchildren

Sinead is of West Indian and Birmingham parentage. She comes here to see her white granddad and her white nanny. I say 'Where are you going now, Sinead?' and she says 'I am going to see my black nanny now'. I think that's very nice, that children

103

can accept colour without any problems whatsoever.

Bryan Kelly, born 1931

Alum Rock

I was born in Alum Rock in 1968. My parents are Irish immigrants. They're both from the country, west of Ireland, County Galway. They bought a house in Alum Rock. Alum Rock in the '60s was one of those areas that the Irish community came to. When I was growing up in the '70s, all your friends were Irish. Every face in my Catholic school was a white face and they were generally sons and daughters of immigrants. They were all the same background. Those same children were the same ones you see in church. They were the same ones when you went to the Rosary Church Community Centre.

Dave Harte, born 1968

Boyfriends

Dad used to say to me 'If you ever brought a black man home, don't even bother coming home'. I remember, one time me and a black friend were talking about our dads and she said 'My dad said exactly the same thing except it was if I bring a white man home'. We had a bit of laugh about that.

Martha McCarron, born 1972

Jewish Identity

We all thought of ourselves as English and I resented being thought of as Jewish, as something different to English. I resented being thought of as a Jew first of all.

Paul Winter, born 1916

Asian Clothes

I didn't start wearing Asian outfits until my mid-twenties which is quite late. My mum, my dad and my grandparents, even though they were quite strict in some ways, they never really pressurised us to wear Asian clothing. Often I would go to other homes and they were asked to wear them all the time. As a child, whenever we went to functions, we always wore Western clothes – dresses, skirts, trousers. We were always very trendy. We didn't have many clothes but what we did have were very trendy.

Avtar Tulwar, born 1969

Fitting in

Because we were brought up over here, I'd say that our culture is diluted and our dialect is different. We go to Cyprus and they don't really understand our accent. We are treated as foreigners when we go to Cyprus as well as over here. It does feel that we've got no real home where we're accepted. I say I'm British of Greek Cypriot descent but I was born in

Birmingham and I am a very, very proud Brummie.

Gabriel Gabriel, born 1963

Irish Music

There was always Irish music in the house, in the car. As a family, we used to go up to the Irish Centre in Digbeth and go and listen to the bands. I loved it as a child. I loved the sense of community – that you were known and that your parents were known. There was that sense of belonging, that makes you feel safe.

Martha McCarron, born 1972

Finding Roots

Our children were both born in Birmingham and have grown up in Birmingham. They have been back to Hong Kong for holiday three times. We deliberately sent them both back to Hong Kong for the summer holidays by themselves. That really helped them to identify and to know that we are Chinese. No matter how integrated, how British our thinking is, in blood, we are Chinese. I think it helped them to find their roots. It gave them the incentive to learn Chinese. Before, no matter how hard we try, they will not learn. They did not see the incentive of learning Chinese, but since then, I could see it changed their attitude. They realised we are Chinese.

Wai Lan Liu, born 1953

Feeling Irish

I feel Irish even though I was born in this country. I don't associate myself with being a Brummie. I feel Irish when I am here but a lot of people don't understand that. If you've grown up with Irish parents who talk to you with an Irish accent, your whole culture is Irish and you associate with Irish people, you do feel Irish. But then when I go over to Ireland, I feel English. I've got a huge family over there. The one family of cousins that we usually stay with, there are five cousins and they've all got red hair like me. I do feel at home when I go there.

Martha McCarron, born 1972

My Community

Growing up in the early '70s, I was born here in England. People say 'Where are you from?' and I say 'I am British. I've got a British passport'. And people say 'No you're not, you're Indian'. I do regard myself as British. I find it annoying when people say 'What community are you from?' I think that is wrong, because to me the community is the environment where I am living. I live in an area where I have got neighbours who are white, Asian, a Scottish person, and an Irish person. To me that is my community. That is the community that I live in.

Gurdip Gill, born 1969

Gurdip Gill aged eight.

Unsettled

Being half German has affected me through my life because to some extent I don't feel settled really. Sometimes I can think of the German word for something before I can think of the English word. I did work in Germany for a couple of years and I learned the language there. Because I've got a Birmingham accent, I do think of myself as a Brummie. When I'm in Birmingham, I think a lot about Germany and when I'm in Germany, I think a lot about England.

Georg Hands, born 1947

Pride

I am proud of being mixed race. I think it's a huge advantage to any children that are mixed race because I've got the advantage of my Asian culture and my white culture. I can choose what religion I want to be, what race I want to think of myself as because I've got the influence of both of them in my life. I have that ability that a single race person wouldn't.

Lara Coles, born 1983

Jewish Religion

My father was very pious. He had his seat in the synagogue because in the synagogue you pay for your own seat. It has a little lid where you keep your prayer book and your prayer shawl. When I was about eleven, I decided to opt out. I refused to be Bar Mitzvahed, much to the sorrow of my mother. I have not practised the religion since then but I am still a Jew. I sometimes very much regret that I have not followed the religion more than I have done.

Paul Winter, born 1916

Going to the Temple

I was brought up as a Sikh. We are a Sikh family. My father's roots are in Punjab. As a child, going to the temple was a ritual which I have carried on for my children. We don't force it on the children. They understand we are Indian, we are Punjabis. Raajan who is five goes with his nan because she goes to the temple three or four times a week. Before I had the children, I stopped going to the temple but I didn't stop believing. When I had the children, I started looking at religion a little bit more. Sometimes when I feel the pressure, I have been to the temple at five or six o'clock in the morning, coming home from work, or maybe when one of the children has been ill. It's a private time to say prayers or just have private thoughts.

Gurdip Gill, born 1969

Greek Orthodox Churches

Our churches are really wonderful with gold icons made out of real gold leaf. The Priest calls them a paradise of colour. We've got two Greek Orthodox churches. We've got one at George Road, Erdington and one in Summer Hill, in Birmingham city centre. I look at the Indian community and the Pakistani community and they have advanced so much. They've got mosques and temples but we've got two only, and we were here first! We should learn off them because they've got a good community spirit amongst them. I think it's up to us second generation and third generation to correct it.

Gabriel Gabriel, born 1963

Ramgariha Sikh Temple, Graham Street, Birmingham.

Finding a New Religion

I was brought up as a Seventh Day
Adventist and we had what was called
Sabbath school as opposed to Sunday
school. It stayed with me and I believed
in it. It was an awfully large part of my
life and then when I was eighteen I
became pregnant and after that, life
changed completely. The people that
we'd heard about every week, the
sinners, I became one of those people
and it wasn't a very nice experience.
The people who are very important to
me in my life now are Muslims.

Malika Ahmed, born 1967

Spirituality

Because my grandparents live so far
away, Hindu religion has not played
a big part in my life but we've been to
India for four months and there I did go
to the temple and that did change me. I
found myself. When you go to India,
you do find yourself because it is very
spiritual. When I'm back at home, I
have no religion. I don't believe in God
and I don't go to the temple.

Lara Coles, born 1983

CHAPTER 7

Dancing through the years

The Locarno Ballroom played host to the television programme, *Come Dancing*, in the late 1950s.

Bryan Kelly (left) worked as a bouncer at the Shamrock Club in Inge Street, 1956.

The Duck's Arse

I used to go dancing on Monday nights at a place called Laura Dixon's on the Dudley Road. Each week I went with a couple of girls that I worked with. It was the time of *Rock Around the Clock* with Bill Haley. Some of the boys were very physical and you could be up in the air. If you were really good and the fellow was really good, you could go through their legs as well. I just used to get giddy and have to go and sit down. The music was very, very exciting. I can remember the boys very well with their teddy boy suits with the trousers and the hair all flicked at the back –

they used to call it the duck's arse.

Norma Morgan, born 1937

Teddy Boys

I was shown a club called the Harp in Walford Road, Sparkbrook. I went along there but I was refused admission because the bouncer on the door pointed at my trousers which he said were too narrow at the bottoms. Of course this was the era of the Teddy Boys and this being an Irish club they seemed to frown on that.

Bryan Kelly, born 1931

Tower Ballroom

I met my husband at the Tower Ballroom in Edgbaston. It was known then as the 'Gay Tower'. We used to wear mini-skirts in the late '60s. I had a friend who had legs up to her armpits, so she could get away with a mini-skirt and she could wear hot pants. We did wear beautiful cocktail dresses. There was the foxtrot and waltz. They did have rock and roll as well but it was a proper general dance on a Saturday night. It was a beautiful ballroom, it really was. The thing that always stuck in my mind was that they had plastic palm trees around the floor. It was really quite elegant.

Mary Cheshire, born 1945

Harry Phillips'

Iwent to my first dance in about 1932 when I was fifteen at a Methodist Sunday school. It was a real stumble round the room with any boy that was foolish enough to ask you to dance. Then I progressed to going to better dances. When I was about twenty, twenty-one, I used to go to the Farcroft Hotel in Rookery Road and that had a proper floor. Then I progressed to going to a place in Aston called Harry Phillips' Albert Hall and there I really learned to dance. I met my husband at that place when I was about twenty-three – and my mother had met my father at that place when they were young. We used to do slow foxtrot, waltz, tango and rumba.

Marjorie Sanders, born 1915

Nightclubbing

When I was sixteen in 1986, Birmingham started to develop. I got incredibly bored by nightclubs. You get there, you have a bit of a dance, you have a bit of a drink and after about an hour or two, I got completely bored and would fall asleep. When I started going into town for a night out there were a few nightclubs that were the place to be seen in. There was the Dome which was a huge nightclub on the Bristol

The Palace Ballroom, High Street, Erdington, 1952.

Henry and Mair Goodhall taught dancing at Highfield Hall, Hall Green during the 1930s.

Road, then there was a place called XLs and there was another nightclub called Faces which was in the Five Ways shopping centre. You had to be eighteen to get into these nightclubs and I started going to clubs when I was sixteen or seventeen. I was terrified of getting found out. So I'd always practise my false date of birth so I wouldn't forget. I even had a postcard that I wrote it on.

Emma Richardson, born 1970

The Golden Ladies

When I was in my early to mid-twenties, round about 1991, Fozzie's was a really good club. It had a very good reputation. I think to improve the image of the club, the owner would park his Rolls Royce outside so you'd think 'Oh, this is a really good place'. The kind of people that went there ranged in age from fourteen year olds, who tried their best to look eighteen and nineteen, and usually succeeded, right up to people who were in their late fifties, early sixties. I suppose it was mainly a black club. The music would range on any given night. You'd get a whole cross-section of reggaes, R'n'B, bit of soul, a little bit of hip hop – but not too much because that's mainly for a younger audience. The men would be in their suits and ties trying to look posh and happy. The ladies would be in tight, tight dresses also trying to look posh and happy. You could tell they couldn't wait to get home to get out of that dress. You'd get what we call the glamour girls at the other extreme. The golden ladies who come in gold jewellery, gold

eyelashes, gold wigs, gold stiletto shoes. So you'd get a total wide variety really. I'd have a tight skimpy dress on and stiletto heels and shiny tights or shiny stockings. It was a good atmosphere and you knew that you could go there on a Saturday night and have a good time.

Malika Ahmed, born 1967

Cliff Richard

In about 1956, Cliff Richard came to Birmingham and he was the sexiest thing you'd ever seen on TV. He was the nearest thing we'd got to Elvis Presley – he did mimic him in a way. He was sexy and we were all absolutely mad on him. My boyfriend was in the police force and part of his patch was around Bingley Hall exhibition centre. I hadn't had enough money to go and see him but I was going on about it. But he said 'That Cliff Richard, I saw him when I was on duty. He'd got a face full of acne and some of them were so bad they needed bursting'. I was devastated and even now when I see Cliff Richard on telly, I have a good look at his skin just in case.

Norma Morgan, born 1937

Disco

From when I was eighteen in 1975, for a whole ten years until I got married, we would use the Tower Ballroom in Edgbaston. The lads were very keen on it, I think the ladies were as well, because it was a popular meeting place for 'discotheque-ing'. They'd have bands on as well. We also used to use the nightclubs in Birmingham town centre – Samantha's, Pollyanna's, Rebecca's, The Locarno. When I was courting my wife, I occasionally took her there and I'd run into friends who'd take the mick out of me because they'd gone there to try and meet new girls. They'd got the attitude that you don't take a girl there that you knew already.

Steve Rogers, born 1957

Club Scene

I went to a nightclub a year or so ago and I was amazed at the club culture now, how it has changed. When I was a teenager, there would be a lot of people smoking. There was certain a way to dress, a fashion of the time and everybody tended to wear that. There was always very middle of the road music on at virtually every place that you went to. But now when you go into a club you are searched for drugs. And some nightclubs they look in the top of a lipstick case just in case somebody's got an 'e' in there. You're very often given a body search now.

Emma Richardson, born 1970

Coffee and Gateau

After we'd been to our rock and roll evening, we used to go to local coffee bars. There was a lovely coffee bar on the Hagley Road opposite the King's Head and when I first met my husband we used to go there a lot. They couldn't have made any money because it was full of seventeen year olds. We could only afford one thing. We used to have a coffee and a slice of gateau, and you really made that last a couple of hours. If you were a really wicked young person, you went to the pub. I didn't ever go in pubs because I hadn't got the courage.

Norma Morgan, born 1937

114

CHAPTER 8

Friends and neighbours

Women wash clothes in Court 6, Hanley Street, in the early 1920s.

New houses in Castle Bromwich, 1953.

Back-to-Backs

We lived in 1 back of 6 Parliament Street, Aston, the house where my father was born in 1912. It was a back-to-back house with one room down, one room on the top and an attic stuck on the top of that. The measurements was roughly ten by twelve. You had no furniture as such and you had no front or back garden. It had single cavity brick walls so you could hear everything that was going on. Not only could you hear the people rowing next door, but you could hear the people rowing two doors away.

Bob Houghton, born 1936

Brewhouse, Toilets and Miskins

The door opened on to a blue brick yard and in the yard was two latrines which were shared by six families. There was a brewhouse where the women washed all the week's clothes. They had to work on a rota system. They had to leave the washhouse clean for the next family to come in and if it was dirty, woe betide them. The toilets were a different matter. They cared dearly about the brewhouse but they didn't care about the toilets. They used to stink and overflow, and they didn't have a door on. Directly next to the toilet were the dustbins which we used to call the miskins. There would be one dustbin for each household and on the dustbin would be painted the number of the house, and woe betide you if you used someone else's dustbin. Because our mum never had a husband to look after her, she was like the butt end of everything, so they would use our dustbin and our mum would cry.

Bob Houghton, born 1936

New House in Castle Bromwich

Me dad got himself signed up for a mortgage. They never said anything to any of the neighbours especially Mabel next door. She used to come round and say 'We're going to have this posh new council flat when we leave the slums'. My mother never said anything even though she was always boasting. My mum and dad had put a deposit down on a brand new house being built in Castle Bromwich. We used to go up every weekend and watch the next stage of the house being built. Eventually the house was completed and my mum got the keys. Before we moved in, mum wanted to give it a clean out and get it measured for curtains. One day we were going to go up to the house, she said to Janet Josephine, the little girl next door, 'Do you want to come out with us?' We went on the bus up to Castle Bromwich and when we got to the house, Janet Josephine said 'Whose house is this?' We said 'It's ours, we've bought it'. We went back to the little slum house in Nechells and Janet Josephine went in and told her mum that my mum and dad had bought a 'palace with a garden'. Her mum went berserk, she couldn't get over it. When we left Lupin Street, they went off to their council flat and my mum and dad went off to their brand new house in Castle Bromwich.

Derek Bennett, born 1947

Chelmsley Wood

They'd started this new housing estate, a new village that was going to be Chelmsley Wood. The rents were £3 15s a week which was astronomical.

Derek Bennett's family moved to Castle Bromwich from Nechells in 1961. New housing estates gave families more space and, for many people, their first house with inside toilet and bathroom.

John and Richard in the Houghton family's house in Chelmsley Wood, 1969. For their parents, it was the first house they had ever lived in with an indoor bathroom.

Chelmsley Wood provided the Houghton family with many new opportunities. The oldest son, Robert, aged ten, stands by a fence among the brand new gardens of the estate.

We decided that we could afford that money. We moved to Chelmsley Wood in wonderful open countryside. The kids loved it, they still live here today. We've been here thirty years. It's got a very bad name but it's no worse than anywhere else. What I liked about Chelmsley Wood was what it offered the children; comprehensive schools, wide open spaces, schools that had their own football pitches, their own swimming pool. It changed our life, it enriched us. I went to see my grandson playing football. It was just like watching my son playing football. It was unbelievable, playing on the same field.

Bob Houghton, born 1936

First Telephone

When I was about five in 1921, we had the very first telephone in Harborne. We had a notice outside the shop which used to say 'You may telephone from here, 2d'. Everybody came to use our telephone. They used to say 'Can we use the telephone but we don't know how to use it so could you use it for us?' So my mother and father used to ring. There was a big handle on it and a big speaker. People got so used to it, they'd ring up at night and say 'Could you go and tell my mother I'm running late, I can't get home tonight'. In the end, we practically turned into messengers.

Stanley Webb, born 1916

25 stone Woman

Next door to me was a widow who was extremely fat, she was at least 25 stone. Outside my house were two steps and she tripped and fell down the steps and broke her ankle. She was waving her legs in the air. My father and everybody went out. She'd got no drawers on. So, they called the ambulance people. The stretcher consisted of two poles and a canvas sheet between them. Well, they tried to pick her up but they couldn't lift her and one of the poles snapped. So they went and got her armchair out of the house, and put her in the armchair. About six of them tried to pick the armchair up with her in it but just as they got to the top of the steps, the arm came off the armchair and the lot of them tumbled back down the steps again.

Alfred Palmerfield, born 1927

Helping Each Other

When I was seven in 1935, we lived in Hamstead Village. If there was a lady and she was going to have a baby, all the ladies gathered round. Those that could knit, knitted for her. Those that could sew would cut an old sheet in half and tack it all around and make sheets for the baby. They would all help when that baby was born. The one who could deliver them the best, that was the one that would go in. The others would do a meal for the husband, clean the house for when the doctor came. By the time the doctor came it was all over. Everybody would go in to see her. They'd all put a penny and give it to the mum. If anyone was ill and died at home someone would go in to lay them out. Then on the day of the funeral, somebody would go in and make sure that there was a table laid so that when the mourners came back they could all have something to eat and everybody in the village would go to the funeral because everybody would know him.

Peggy Gilbert, born 1928

Grocer's Delivery

A job I had when I was about ten or eleven was for a local greengrocer, using the old family pram. I said 'Would you like me to offer a delivery service to your customers for greengrocery?' So she said 'Yes, we'll try it'. She put the orders in baskets and I used to dash off with this pram. Once I was out of sight of this woman, I used to sit on the side of the pram and scoot down and deliver all this greengrocery. I used to get tips.

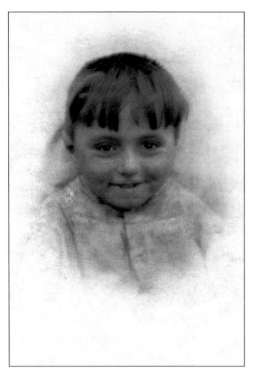

Alfred Palmerfield aged five in 1932 while his family were living in Newtown Row.

Sometimes I would get a great big lump of bread pudding. I went out one day and I tipped the lot over. Well, my mother had brought me up to share everything. What I did, everything that was lying all over the road, I shared it all out, equally in each basket, and nobody said a word.

Dan Jones, born 1929

Shelling Peas

When you came out of the houses, most of the women used to sit on the step to peel the potatoes or shell peas so that they could talk to their next door neighbour. They talked about everybody else and they knew everybody's business. There was no chance of anybody hiding anything. They were soon found out. The step was a very important part of the house. People used to judge the state of the step. If the step was dirty then they reckoned the house was dirty, so the step would be kept immaculately clean.

Alfred Palmerfield, born 1927

Knowing the Beat

In 1956, I joined the Birmingham City Police. I went to Ladywood and that was when I first went on to the beat. The first thing we did, we had to work a month on nights to learn the area. You just went round and round and round, looking at street names so that you knew your area. After that month, you were expected to know every street. Before we went out on the streets every day, we used to look at the rogues gallery. In the parade room, there was a big dart board case full of photographs and you got to know who they were and where they lived. Then you could go out on to the street and let them know that you knew who they were, even though you were a young fresh-faced bobby.

Policeman, born 1937

Burglary

Mugging or burglary was unheard of. For one thing, nobody had got anything to pinch. Plus if you was a burglar, you'd soon be found out. If they found you were the burglar, then the

120

neighbours would come round and give you a good hiding.

Alfred Palmerfield, born 1927

Crime

There was crime years ago. People say 'When people had nothing, there wasn't so much crime' but that isn't true, there was crime. It wasn't safe to leave your door open. There was crime probably because there was more poverty and more need for crime.

Paul Winter, born 1916

Special Attentions

When people went on holiday, they used to put their house on the Special Attention list. The bobby was supposed to go round there during his tour of duty to check the house. In the summer months, when there was a lot of people away, that used to be one special tour of duty. You'd have a pushbike and you'd go all round the Special Attentions. One day, I went to a house to do a Special Attention and there was a pedal cycle at the front and I recognised it as one of my colleague's bikes so I opened the gate very quietly, and I walked round the back and he's sitting in a deckchair in the back garden reading the *Sports Argus*. And I said 'Hello!' and he jumped so high that the

A Birmingham policeman demonstrates the radio in his patrol car.

chair collapsed underneath him and he chased me for three-quarters of a mile round the streets of Edgbaston.

Policeman, born 1937

Looking for a Fight

On a Friday and a Saturday, the men used to get drunk and they wanted to fight. There was one chap who lived on the end of my row of houses who used to get drunk every Friday night. He used to come down banging on the doors and shout 'Come out and fight'. Him being a man of 6' 6", with shoulders like an ox, nobody went out to fight him.

Alfred Palmerfield, born 1927

Fighting

Sometimes you'd get reports of a fight but in those days there was only three cars on the division and if they were dealing with something else, by the time we'd walked, the fights were generally over. It was the same with domestic violence. We used to get reports coming in of a man and wife having a heated argument and because we'd got no radios, the only way the station could get that information to you was by either sending another constable who happened to be in the station or put on the flashing police pillar.

Policeman, born 1937

Police Radios

In the late 1960s, I was a sergeant at Cotteridge police station where radios were introduced for the first time. It was a great innovation because instead of going to a phone box or asking somebody if you could use their phone, at the press of a button you could get assistance. I was one of the first officers to take a radio out and I got to the corner of Pershore Road and Watford Road and all I could hear was interference, just noise. And this little old lady came up to me and she says 'Can you understand what that is saying?' And I said 'Yes, of course Madam, it's all in code!'

Policeman, born 1937

CHAPTER 9

Birmingham pub bombings:
a survivor's story

The bar of the Mulberry Bush pub after the bombings on 21 November 1974, where 10 people were
killed and 40 injured.

The story of Wendy Turner, born 1956

It was just after Christmas in 1973 and my boyfriend got a job at the Tavern in the Town. On my eighteenth birthday in February 1974, he got me a job at the Tavern. I got married in August 1974. We went on our honeymoon and we came back in the October. We had been back at work three weeks and that's when the bombing happened.

On the 21 November 1974, we went to work as normal. I had arranged to swap my shift with a part-timer called Thomas. He was a student and was about eighteen or nineteen. It also meant changing positions on the bar because we had three positions on the bar with three tills. I arrived at work at about seven o'clock that evening and I took up my position in the centre.

It was just a normal, happy, busy atmosphere. The Three Degrees were playing on the Juke Box – *When Will I See You Again*. Then there was a sudden shake and a loud noise, lights flickered and shook. A lot of us guessed that it must have been a bomb that's gone off somewhere. One of the barmaids said 'Wouldn't it be great if we had a bomb scare and we could all go home'. Within two minutes of her saying that, we had a bomb go off in our own pub.

Words couldn't describe what it was like. There was this huge blast of light that is like fifty times worse than looking at the sun. I had to put my hands over my face. I didn't hear a thing. The next thing I knew, there was a man in front of me who I'd been serving and he turned. And that was the last thing I saw. I was holding a glass and I dropped it. I thought 'Oh my God, I've broke this glass'. I dropped to my knees and I curled up in the foetal position and all this debris and wood just kept falling on top of me and I felt like I was being buried.

After, it was so quiet. It was dark, black. I was lying there. I knew I was fully conscious. I knew what had happened and I thought 'I'm dead'. Then I thought 'Perhaps if I scream, I might get a response from somebody'. Someone shouted back 'Shut up, you stupid cow, there might be another bomb'. I just lay quiet then. I could feel something in my leg and I actually was convinced I had lost it. Time had no significance. I saw flashlights through gaps through the rubble. I managed to put my hand through to attract attention and these firemen lifted me out. I was still terrified to stand up. I was frightened to look. They took me round where the bar was and I had to step over people. The place was covered in blood. It was stained up the walls and you would catch glimpses of it in the flashlights. It was chaos. It is something that you would never be prepared for. After they pulled me out of the rubble, it was very difficult to see. There was just a carpet of people just lying all over the floor. There was an awful lot of blood on the floor. You would see people with serious injuries. You'd hear whining and groaning.

There was one thing that saved my life was the fact that we had these

The entrance of the Tavern in the Town, New Street, Birmingham, 21 November 1974. In the Tavern, 11 people were killed by the blast and 126 injured.

concrete blocks which were pillars. There was that between me and the bomb and I truly believe that if that hadn't been there, I wouldn't be here.

They took everybody they could on stretchers out the back exit because there were no windows in this pub so the blast was contained. Taxis and cars were taking people to hospital and these cars were covered in blood but they kept coming back for more people. We were taken to the General.

It was only then that I realised what had happened and that was when the shock started. Everybody was shaking. That's how I was for two weeks, I couldn't stop shaking. There was an awful lot of confusion. I was actually stitched up. I was absolutely covered with blood from head to toe. I'd got lots of shattered glass in my head and my husband was also working that night and he was blown through the cellar wall, banged his head and he had severe concussion. He was never

Damage to shops on New Street after the Birmingham pub bombings, 21 November 1974.

actually treated as he just had bruising so he was overlooked.

The minute I got out of the hospital, there was photographers flashing with their cameras. I just instinctively put my hands to my face again and I just cried and they chased me and followed me to this car. I was just bundled into the car. They were asking what I thought about the IRA and I just couldn't answer. The driver whisked me away and took me home.

My mother had been sitting at home, listening to a newsflash saying that the Tavern in the Town had been blown up and she was convincing herself that I was off that night. Desperately they tried to make phone calls but all the lines were busy. My father tried to get into town by car and all the roads had been sealed off. The whole family came down to my parents' house. When I got home it was very tearful, it was the happiest reunion. It was very sad.

Thomas, I found out, did die in hospital very shortly after from third degree burns to his body. They couldn't even get his clothes off him because they were welded to him like plastic. This shocked me because I knew that it should have been me that night, working in the position that he was working. Until today that haunts me. I've never forgotten his name. A few years ago, they erected a memorial to all the victims that died in the Tavern and the Mulberry Bush. I couldn't bring myself to attend the ceremony but my boyfriend did take me to see it. I saw Thomas' name and actually seeing it written on the stone really, really got to me and I burst into tears.

My father took me back the very next morning because he wanted to see for himself the devastation and to retrieve any of my belongings. He cannot believe how anybody got out of there alive. He even cried himself.

After that I couldn't settle. I couldn't rest. I couldn't relate. If a car backfired, I'd fall to my knees. If somebody had left a bag unattended, it would frighten me to death. The relationship with my husband became very strained. He underwent a personality change. He went from being a very quiet, passive, happy-go-lucky man to obsessive behaviour. He became violent. He started hitting me. Once a month he would hit me, then it was once a week, then it became like everyday. The relationship became so strained that I feared for my own life and I knew that the marriage had to end. It broke my marriage irretrievably because of the effect that the bomb had

The front of the Mulberry Bush after the bombings.

Wendy Turner aged twenty in 1976, two years after the Birmingham pub bombings.

on my husband, because of the head injuries. He never had any counselling or received any help at all. We were unable to work. I wasn't earning any money. I was very unsettled.

I hated going in to town. I am absolutely petrified of balloons and party poppers as a result of what happened to me on that night. They frighten me to death.

I did have a letter from the Criminal Injuries Compensation board. We had to go to an interview to assess how they thought we were psychologically affected. By the time we went it was several months later and all the wounds had healed but psychologically they hadn't healed. A few months later, I was given £200 from the Compensation Board. They actually awarded me £650 and £30 for costs for loss of belongings. They gave me £200 up front and fifteen months later, I received the other £480 and that's what they thought I was worth.